WINES

OF

ITALY

VINO

THE QUALITY OF LIFE

D1402208

BY BURTON ANDERSON

Published by the Italian Institute for Foreign Trade/ICE
Sponsored by the Italian Ministry of Agricultural, Food and Forestry Resources
© The Italian Trade Commission, New York, 1994
The text was written by Burton Anderson
Editing UNION DESIGN Srl - Rome
Third Edition

TABLE OF CONTENTS

*I*taly's growing reputation with wine is due not only to the fact that it produces and exports more than any other country but that it offers the greatest variety of types, ranging through nearly every color, flavor and style imaginable.

In the past it was sometimes said that Italians kept their best wines to themselves while supplying foreign markets with tasty but anonymous vino in economy sized bottles. But markets have changed radically over the last couple of decades as consumers in many lands—notably in Italy itself—have insisted on better quality.

In response to demand, Italian producers have moved rapidly to the forefront of enology, improving techniques to create wines of undeniable class in every region, north and south. Their wines derive not only from native vines, which represent an enormous array, but also from a growing range of international varieties.

For a while it may have seemed that the worldwide trend to standardize vines and wines was bound to compromise Italy's role as the champion of diversity. But, instead, leading producers in many parts of the country have kept the emphasis firmly on traditional vines. They have taken the authentic treasures of their ancient land and enhanced them in modern wines whose aromas and flavors are not to be experienced anywhere else. Getting to know the unique wines of Italy is an endless adventure in taste.

Experts have increasingly proclaimed Italy's premier wines among the world's finest. Many of the noblest originate in the 240 zones officially classified as DOC or DOCG, but a number of individualistic wines go proudly under their own titles. Yet consumers abroad, perhaps unaware of the wealth of types (or perhaps overwhelmed by the numbers) have not always taken advantage of this unmatchable variety.

This booklet provides a basic reference to the wines of Italy through a survey of the 20 regions. It begins in the south, in those sunny Mediterranean places that the ancient Greeks came to call Oenotria, the land of wine, and moves north through the historic hills past Rome and Florence and over the Apennines to the Po valley and the Alps, with some of Europe's highest vineyards.

There is vital if brief information on each region's geography and climate, production figures, grape varieties, traditions and trends, along with a listing and abbreviated description of practically every wine that matters. There are also notes on Italy's wine laws and how to read a label, as well as a glossary of terms and references to books for deeper reading. The booklet is designed to be compact enough to carry around yet thorough enough to answer questions that might arise while selecting, serving or tasting wines.

A final feature discusses Italian food, the cucina Italiana which has become the preferred way of eating in much of the world today. From the vast array of regional dishes, it selects certain specialties and suggests wines to drink with them.

ITALIAN WINE THROUGH THE AGES

*I*taly's modern prodigiousness with wine scarcely begins to tell the story of its people's perennial links to the vine. The nature of the place — the influence of Mediterranean sunshine and mountain air currents on the hillsides of the elongated peninsula and islands — favors what seems to be an almost spontaneous culture of wine.

The heritage dates back some 4,000 years to when prehistoric peoples pressed wild grapes into juice that, as if by magic, fermented into wine. The ancient Greeks, expanding into Italy's southern reaches, dubbed the colonies Oenotria, the land of wine. Etruscans were subtle and serene practitioners of the art of winemaking in the hills of central Italy, as attested by the art and artifacts left in their spacious tombs.

The Romans propagated the cult of Bacchus to all corners of the empire, developing a flourishing trade in wine throughout the Mediterranean and beyond. So sophisticated was their knowledge of viticulture and enology that their techniques were not equalled again until the 17th or 18th centuries when Italians and other Europeans began to regard the making of wine as science rather than mystique.

Winemaking in Italy advanced rapidly through the 19th century, as methods of vinification and aging were improved and the use of corks to seal reinforced bottles and flasks permitted orderly shipping of wine worldwide. Such names as Chianti, Barolo and Marsala became known in Europe and beyond.

A century ago several Italian wines were recognized as among the finest of their type: mainly Piedmontese and Tuscan reds from the Nebbiolo and Sangiovese varieties, but also white wines, still and sparkling, dry or sweet, merited international respect. Growers had complemented their local varieties with foreign vines, such as Cabernet, Merlot and the Pinots. There was evidence, then as now, that Italy's climate and terrain favored vines of many different types, and consumers elsewhere in Europe and in North America had come to appreciate these new examples of class.

Then came phylloxera and other scourges to devastate Europe's vineyards around the turn of the century. Italian growers, who had been working with thousands of local varieties, were forced to reduce the numbers. Many opted for newly developed, more productive clones of both native and foreign vines. Taking advantage of the long, sunny growing season, they forced yields up, reasoning that there was usually more profit to be made from quantity than quality.

Through the hard times of wars and depression, Italy became one of the world's leading purveyors of low cost wine, often sold in containers of outlandish shapes and sizes. Though such practices were profitable for some, they did little for the image of Italian wine abroad.

For decades responsible producers had been trying to tighten regulations and put the emphasis on premium quality. But it was not until the denominazione d'origine laws were passed nearly 30 years ago that a new climate of dignity and trust was created, providing the basis for what came to be known as the modern renaissance in Italian wine.

Since Vernaccia di San Gimignano became the first DOC in 1966, the list has grown to include 240 zones delimited geographically within which a multitude of wines are controlled for authenticity. (See details under Wine Laws and Labels.) Yet the officially classified wines represent only 12 to 15 percent of the total. Beyond DOC and DOCG are thousands of others: local wines, opportunistic blends with imaginative names, and a growing number of admirable individual efforts that qualify as commercial rather than homemade.

Despite the reduction through this century, Italy still has more types of vines planted than any other country, both the natives and a virtually complete range of the so-called international varieties. The number of officially approved Viitis vinifera vines runs well into the hundreds, and there are even a few non-vinifera varieties and hybrids used here and there by the nation's countless do-it-yourself winemakers.

This heritage of vines permits Italy to produce a greater range of distinctive wines than any other nation. Though Italy is most noted for its noble reds for aging, trends favor more immediate types of rosso, including the vini novelli to be drunk within months of the harvest. White wine production is growing, in both lightweight styles and bianco of greater substance and depth. Italy is a major producer of bubbly wines, whether in the lightly fizzy frizzante or the fully sparkling spumante made by either the sealed tank charmat or bottle fermented classico method.

This wealth of wines may seem overwhelming. Consumers outside Italy are sometimes bewildered by the assortment of names of places, grape varieties, proprietors and types and in exasperation turn to more comprehensible sources for wine.

This booklet is designed to provide readers with clear cut information that should allay some of the confusion. But it cannot offer simple solutions to the mastery of Italian wines. That can come only through experience, as wine drinkers overcome taste prejudices and the fear of the unknown and come to appreciate the advantages of being different in an age of uniformity. To the adventurous, Italian wines offer a whole galaxy of aromas and flavors.

Without staking claims to supremacy, it seems fair to submit that numerous Italian wines stand with the international elite. But what is perhaps most encouraging in an era of crisis for wine the world over is that Italy's premium production continues to improve. Producers and consumers alike have come to realize that these days in wine it is character that counts and quality that pays, and Italians have become increasingly committed to delivering both.

*I*talians over the centuries have pioneered laws to control the origins and protect the names of wines. The ancient Romans defined production areas for dozens of wines. In 1716, the Grand Duchy of Tuscany delimited the zones for important wines, setting a precedent for modern legislation.

Yet only since the mid-1960s have controls been applied nationwide to wines of "particular reputation and worth" under what is known as denominazione di origine controllata or, by the initials, as DOC. There are now about 240 DOCs, all delimited geographically. Wines from 13 zones have been further distinguished as DOCG (the G for garantita or guaranteed authenticity). These are Barbaresco, Barolo, Brunello di Montalcino, Chianti (in seven subzones), Vino Nobile di Montepulciano, Albana di Romagna, Gattinara, Carmignano (red only), Torgiano Rosso riserva, Taurasi, Montefalco Sagrantino, Vernaccia di San Gimignano and Moscato d'Asti/Asti Spumante.

Within the DOC and DOCG zones more than 900 types of wine are produced. They may be defined by color or type (still, bubbly or sparkling; dry, semisweet or sweet; natural or fortified). Or they may be referred to by grape variety (e.g. Trentino DOC with 17 varietals in its 20 subcategories). Or by age (young as novello or aged as vecchio, stravecchio or riserva). Or by a special subzone as classico or superiore. The latter may also apply to a higher degree of alcohol or a longer period of aging, though use of the term superiore will be increasingly restricted. (Most definitions can be found in the Glossary).

Sweeping changes in the wine laws in 1992 opened the way for DOC and DOCG wines to carry names of communities, areas of geographical or historical importance in the zones and names of individual vineyards of established reputation. Such wines may also carry the European Community designation of VQPRD or VSQPRD (for spumante), VFQPRD (for frizzante) or VLQPRD (for liquoroso or fortified).

Yet in recent times DOC and DOCG have accounted for only 12 to 15 percent of Italy's production. Some unclassified wines may be referred to as spumante or frizzante or as amabile or dolce (for sweet) or as liquoroso, but the majority of dry, still wines had to be labeled as vino da tavola. In its simplest versions such table wine can specify color but no vintage, grape variety or place

name. More specific were table wines with geographical indications, such as Rosso di Toscana or Tocai del Veneto.

But now, thanks to the new laws of 1992, much of the better vino da tavola is expected to qualify under the category of Indicazione geografica tipica (IGT), designed to officially classify wines by color or grape varieties and typology from large areas. IGT will be the Italian equivalent to the French Vin de pays and German Landwein.

The aim is to increase the proportion of classified wines to a majority of national production, but it is important to remember that many good to excellent Italian wines are still not classified. The reason might be that vineyards are in a non-DOC area or that the wine has been made under a new formula or that the producer chose to retain an individual identity. In the end, the most reliable guide to the quality of any wine from anywhere is the reputation of the individual producer or estate. Certain names are worth getting to know.

Labels must carry the wine's generic name and status (DOC, IGT, Vino da tavola, etc.), the producer's name and location, alcohol by percentage of volume, as well as the net contents in milliliters (with an e as an EEC approved measure). Most DOCG and DOC wines must carry a vintage date. Italian wines imported into the United States must carry the INE seal of approval for export on a red neck label, the term Product of Italy, a description such as "Red table wine" and the importer's name and location.

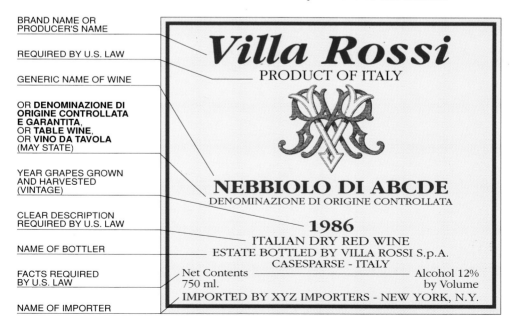

BRAND NAME OR
PRODUCER'S NAME

REQUIRED BY U.S. LAW

GENERIC NAME OF WINE

OR **DENOMINAZIONE DI ORIGINE CONTROLLATA E GARANTITA**,
OR **TABLE WINE**,
OR **VINO DA TAVOLA**
(MAY STATE)

YEAR GRAPES GROWN AND HARVESTED (VINTAGE)

CLEAR DESCRIPTION REQUIRED BY U.S. LAW

NAME OF BOTTLER

FACTS REQUIRED BY U.S. LAW

NAME OF IMPORTER

Villa Rossi

PRODUCT OF ITALY

NEBBIOLO DI ABCDE

DENOMINAZIONE DI ORIGINE CONTROLLATA

1986

ITALIAN DRY RED WINE

ESTATE BOTTLED BY VILLA ROSSI S.p.A.

CASESPARSE - ITALY

Net Contents ———————— Alcohol 12%
750 ml.   by Volume

IMPORTED BY XYZ IMPORTERS - NEW YORK, N.Y.

The following Italian terms may be found on labels or literature about wine.

Abboccato - Lightly sweet.
Alcool - Alcohol, usually stated by % of volume.
Amabile - Semisweet.
Annata - Vintage year.
Azienda agricola or **agraria** or **vitivinicola** - Farm or estate which may not purchase more than half the grapes for wine sold under its labels.
Bianco - White.
Botte - Cask or barrel.
Bottiglia - Bottle.
Brut - Dry.
Cantina - Cellars or winery.
Cantina sociale - Cooperative winery.
Casa vinicola or **azienda vinicola** - Wine house or merchant (commerciante) whose bottlings come mainly from purchased grapes or wines.
Cascina - Farmhouse, often used for estate.
Cerasuolo - Cherry-hued rosé.
Chiaretto - Deep rosé.
Classico - The historic center of a DOC zone.
Consorzio - Consortium of producers.
Dolce - Sweet.
Enoteca - Wine library, public or commercial.
Etichetta - Label.
Fattoria - Farm or estate.
Fermentazione naturale - Natural CO_2 in bubbly wine.
Frizzante or **Frizzantino** - Fizzy or faintly fizzy.
Imbottigliata - Bottled (**all'origine** implies at the source)
Indicazione geografica tipica (IGT) - Recent category to officially classify wines, usually of whole provinces or large areas.
Invecchiato - Aged.
Liquoroso - Strong wine, often fortified with distilled alcohol, though sometimes strength is natural.
Macerazione carbonica - Carbonic maceration, a partial fermentation process of whole grapes in sealed containers under pressure of their self-generated carbon dioxide gas, is used mainly

for vino novello.

Maso - A holding, often referring to a vineyard or estate.

Masseria - Farm or estate.

Metodo Charmat - Sparkling wine by the sealed tank method

Metodo classico or **tradizionale** - Terms for sparkling wine made by the bottle fermentation method, classico or tradizionale replacing champenois or champenoise, which can no longer be used in Italy.

Passito or passita - Partially dried grapes and the strong, usually sweet wines made from them.

Podere - Small farm or estate.

Produttore - Producer.

Recioto -Wine made from partly dried grapes, often sweet and strong.

Riserva - Reserve, for DOC or DOCG wine aged a specified time.

Rosato - Rosé.

Rosso - Red.

Secco - Dry.

Semisecco - Medium sweet, usually in sparkling wine.

Spumante - Sparkling wine, dry or sweet.

Superiore - In DOC wines denotes higher level of alcohol or aging or special geographical origin.

Tenuta - Farm or estate.

Uva - Grape.

Vecchio - Old, to describe aged DOC wines; **Stravecchio**, very old, applies to the longest aged Marsala and to some spirits.

Vendemmia - Harvest or vintage.

Vigna or **vigneto** - Vineyard.

Vignaiolo/Viticoltore - Terms for grape grower.

Vino da tavola - Table wine, applies loosely to most non-DOCs.

Vino novello - New wine, usually red, that must be bottled within the year of harvest.

Vitigno - Vine or grape variety.

Vivace - Lively, as in lightly bubbly wines.

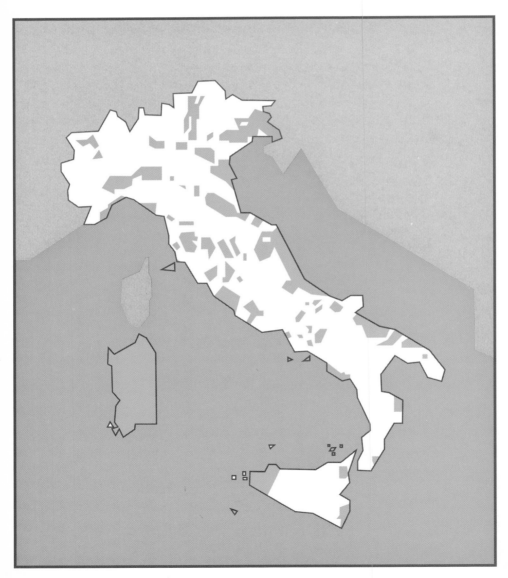

MEDIUM BODIED RED WINES
FULL BODIED RED WINES

*T*he following survey of the wines of Italy's 20 regions follows a geographical pattern which divides the country into four sections: The South and Islands; Central regions; North Central and Northwest regions; Northeast regions. Similarities often exist within these sections in terms of climate and geography, as well as in grape varieties and viticultural and enological practices. But the divisions are rather arbitrary, designed more to aid the reader's orientation than to point up clear distinctions. Italian wines are most accurately perceived region by region.

Each of the 20 regions is a political entity with certain powers of its own in balance with national laws. Every region is further divided into provinces which take the name of a principal city or town. A capsule introduction to each region lists the capital and provinces, size and population, vineyard area and production and rank in each category. There is also a listing, first of DOC or DOCG wines and then of non-classified wines. Since a great deal of information needed to be packed into limited space, each wine is described through abbreviations which follow this key:

R	-	Red *(rosso)*
W	-	White *(bianco)*
P	-	Pink *(rosato, rosé, chiaretto, cerasuolo)*
Dr	-	Dry *(secco, brut)*
Sw	-	Sweet or semisweet *(dolce, amabile, abboccato)*
Sp	-	Sparkling (spumante)
Fz	-	Fizzy or faintly bubbly *(frizzante, frizzantino, vivace)*
Ft	-	Fortified *(liquoroso)*
Rs	-	Reserve *(riserva)*
Sup -		Superior *(superiore,* in reference to higher alcohol, longer aging or a specific zone)
Ag	-	Aging, as required by DOC or DOCG in number of years

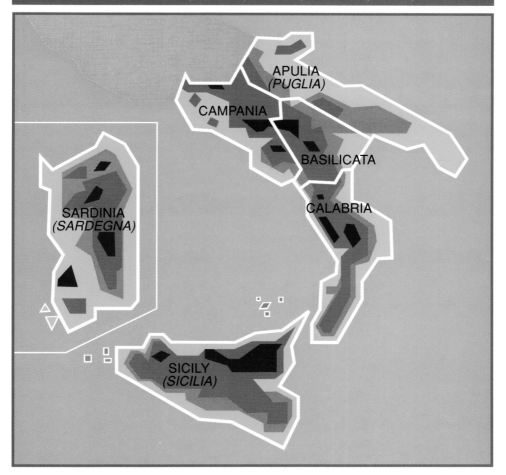

*T*he six regions of Italy's south take in the sunwashed vineyards that prompted the ancient Greeks to nickname their colonies Oenotria. From Hellas they brought to Magna Graecia vines which are still planted today, under such names as Aglianico, Greco, Malvasia, Gaglioppo and Moscato.

The Romans in their turn recognized the potential of the slopes that gave them Falernum, Caecubum, Mamertinum and other heady wines that were eulogized by poets from Horace to Virgil. Pliny the Elder and Columella were among those who recorded methods of viticulture and oenology that included descriptions of

17

how to age and preserve wine and even to make it bubbly. But wine had its ups and downs under the Romans, too, reaching a low point when the Emperor Domitian ordered vines removed and restricted trade to combat excess production.

Many outsiders left their marks on these Mediterranean shores. Foremost among them were the Spaniards, who dominated until the Risorgimento and brought vines into Sardinia, Sicily and other places centuries after the Arabs and Phoenicians planted what may have been the first "foreign" vines in Italy.

It might be argued that at times in the past the vineyards of the Italian Mezzogiorno were put to better use than they have been in recent times. Sicily and Apulia vie for leadership among the 20 regions in volume produced, much of it in the blending wines shipped to northerly places or in bulk wines distilled into industrial alcohol. Though the six regions produce about 40 percent of Italy's total wine, they account for less than 7 percent of the DOC. Yet, after decades in which the emphasis had been steadfastly on quantity, producers in all regions have become increasingly convinced that the future lies in quality, as the volume steadily decreases.

The notion that Italy's south is suited only to the production of hot-blooded wines is neither fair nor accurate. Studied techniques of grape growing and methods of temperature controlled fermentation and storage in oxygen-free conditions have permitted production of dry, balanced wines that can be attractively light and fruity. Several of Italy's most impressive red wines for long aging originate in the south. And there has been a

welcome trend to upgrade the quality and status of the traditional sweet wines from Moscato and Malvasia, as well as Sicily's fortified Marsala and Sardinia's Vernaccia di Oristano.

An unfortunate misconception has it that the Mezzogiorno has a torrid climate, when in fact much of the territory is temperate and parts are downright chilly. Conditions depend on altitude and proximity to the Tyrrhenian, Ionian or Adriatic seas. Some good wines are made in relatively hot places—the slopes of Vesuvius, the isle of Ischia, Apulia's Salento peninsula, Sicily's western coast and Sardinia's Campidano. But many wines of scope come from higher, cooler places—the hills around Avellino in Campania, Basilicata's Vulture, Sicily's Etna and central highlands, Apulia's interior plateau and Sardinia's eastern coastal range.

Each of the six regions has an abundance of hills with conditions considered ideal for modern viticulture. The challenge is to put them to their best use.

Sicily *(SICILIA)*

Regional capital: Palermo

Provinces: Agrigento, Caltanissetta, Catania, Enna, Messina, Palermo, Ragusa, Siracusa, Trapani.

Sicily is Italy's largest region (25,708 square kilometers) and ranks 4th in population (5,084,000).

Vineyards cover 164,500 hectares (1st) of which registered DOC plots total 21,000 ha (5th).

Annual wine production of 11,100,000 hectoliters (2nd to Apulia) includes 2.5% or 277,000 hectoliters DOC (11th), of which more than 95% is white.

*C*ontrasts are not the least of those things in which Sicily abounds. So perhaps it is not surprising that this ancient island boasts one of Italy's most modern wine industries or that a region noted chiefly in the past for strong and often sweet amber Marsala and Moscato has rapidly switched the emphasis toward lighter, dryer wines—whites and reds.

Sicily, the largest Mediterranean island, has more vineyards for wine than any other region. Production in recent years has reached awesome levels—frequently the greatest in volume among the regions. The westernmost province of Trapani alone turns out more wine than the entire regions of Tuscany or Piedmont or such wine nations as Hungary, Austria or Chile. But the proportion of DOC wine in Sicily's total is a mere 2.5% and a major share of that is Marsala, which with some 22 million liters a year ranks among Italy's top ten DOCs in volume.

Marsala, which was devised by English merchant traders nearly two centuries ago, has remained Sicily's proudest wine despite decades of degradation when it was flavored with various syrups and sweeteners. Recently it has enjoyed a comeback with connoisseurs, who favor the dry Marsala Vergine and Superiore Riserva with their warmly complex flavors that rank then with the finest fortified wines of Europe.

The only other DOC wine made in significant quantity in Sicily (about 2.5 million liters a year) is the pale white, bone dry Bianco d'Alcamo. Moscato di Pantelleria, from the remote isle off the coast of Tunisia, is among the richest and most esteemed of Italian sweet wines in the Naturale and Passito Extra versions. Malvasia delle Lipari, from the volcanic Aeolian isles, is a dessert wine as exquisite as it is rare.

The dry white and red wines of Etna, whose vines are draped over the lower slopes of the volcano, can show notable class, as can the pale red but potent Cerasuolo di Vittoria. Production of the other DOCs—the dry, red Faro and the sweet Moscatos of Noto and Siracusa—has been virtually nonexistent in recent times.

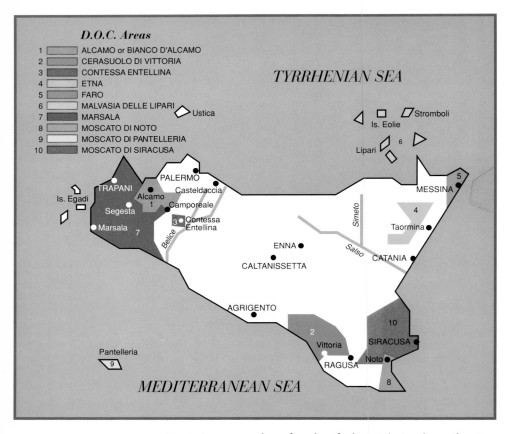

D.O.C. Areas

1. ALCAMO or BIANCO D'ALCAMO
2. CERASUOLO DI VITTORIA
3. CONTESSA ENTELLINA
4. ETNA
5. FARO
6. MALVASIA DELLE LIPARI
7. MARSALA
8. MOSCATO DI NOTO
9. MOSCATO DI PANTELLERIA
10. MOSCATO DI SIRACUSA

TYRRHENIAN SEA

Ustica

Stromboli
Is. Eolie
Lipari

PALERMO
Is. Egadi
TRAPANI
Alcamo
Casteldaccia
MESSINA
Segesta
Camporeale
Marsala
Contessa
Entellina
Taormina
ENNA
CATANIA
CALTANISSETTA
AGRIGENTO
Vittoria
SIRACUSA
Pantelleria
RAGUSA
Noto

MEDITERRANEAN SEA

By contrast, a number of unclassified *vini da tavola* are thriving. Increasingly prominent are the pale, faintly scented, delicately fruity whites which derive largely from native grapes such as Inzolia, Catarratto and Grecanico. Such outsiders as Sauvignon and Chardonnay have also proved promising. Certain reds have achieved prominence, too, mainly those from such admired native varieties as Nero d'Avola (or Calabrese) and Nerello Mascalese and Perricone (or Pignatello).

The most admired brands of Sicilian table wines—Corvo-Duca di Salaparuta and Regaleali—do not qualify under any DOC. Yet Corvo's consistent quality in dry whites and reds from grapes selected throughout the island has made them prizewinners at home and abroad. Regaleali from the Tasca d'Almerita family estate high in the island's central hills, has been producing white, rosé and reds that have won international acclaim.

The Region of Sicily distinguishes wines of consistent quality—whether DOC or not—with a Q, which appears on labels as a seal of approval.

Sicilian wine has not enjoyed universal success, however. In an era of dwindling consumption worldwide, much of the island's production is either shipped away as blending wine or designated for distillation into industrial alcohol.

The region's wine production—four-fifths of which is centered in cooperatives—has been gradually reduced as new emphasis has been given to premium quality. New methods of viticulture in the sunny, temperate hills are helping to realize wines of real character and individuality. Sicily has taken the lead in wine-making in the modern south as producers seem increasingly determined to live up to the promise that was so well known to the ancient Greeks.

DOCs (10)

Alcamo or Bianco d'Alcamo	W-Dr
Cerasuolo di Vittoria	R-Dr
Contessa Entellina W-Dr, also Chardonnay W-Dr; Grecanico W-Dr; Sauvignon Blanc W-Dr	
Etna	R-P-W-Dr
Faro	R-Dr, Ag-1
Malvasia delle Lipari	W-Sw, also Ft
Marsala	W, also R/Dr/Sw-Ft (Fine Ag-1; Superiore Ag-2, Rs Ag-4; Vergine or Soleras Ag-5, Rs or Stravecchio Ag-10), also Cremovo Zabaione W/Sw-Ft or R/Sw-Ft
Moscato di Noto	W-Sw, also Sp, Ft
Moscato di Pantelleria	Naturale W-Sw, also Sp, Ft; Passito W-Sw, also Ft; Passito Extra W-Sw, also Ft, Ag-1
Moscato di Siracusa W-Sw-Ft	

OTHER WINES OF NOTE

Red-Dry	*White-Dry*	*Others*
Cellaro	Bianco di Valguarnera	Conti d'Almerita Brut, W-Dr-Sp
Cerdèse Rosso	Cellaro Bianco	Inzolia di Samperi, W-Sw
Duca Enrico	Cerdèse Bianco	Stravecchio Siciliano, R-Dr-Ft
Libecchio	Corvo Colomba Platino	Vecchio Samperi, W-Dr-Ft
Menfi Rosso	Corvo Prima Goccia	Villa Fontane Solicchiato Bianco W-Sw-Ft
Nerello Siciliano	Donnafugata Vigna di Gabri	
Rapitalà Rosso	Libecchio	
Regaleali Rosso del Conte	Menfi Bianco	
Rubilio	Regaleali Nozze d'Oro	
Terre d'Agala	Rincione	
	Terre di Ginestra	
	Verdello Siciliano	

Sardinia *(SARDEGNA)*

Regional capital: Cagliari

Provinces: Cagliari, Nuoro, Oristano, Sassari.

Sardinia ranks 3rd in size among the regions (24,090 square kilometers) and 12th in population (1,638,000).

Vineyards cover 65,900 hectares (7th) of which registered DOC plots total 7,400 hectares (13th).

Annual wine production of 2,185,000 hectoliters (11th) includes 2.5% or 104,000 hectoliters DOC (14th), of which about 65% is white.

*I*solation in mid-Mediterranean has made Sardinia the most idiosyncratic of Italian regions. Its history has been influenced as much by foreigners — Spaniards in particular — as by other Italians.

The island's vines tell a story of their own, frequently with a Spanish accent. The Mediterranean stalwarts are there in the various clones of Muscat and Malvasia, but several other varieties are practically unique in Italy, such as Girò, Cannonau, Nuragus, Monica, Torbato and Vernaccia di Oristano.

Sardinia's major vineyard area is the Campidano, the fertile plains and low, rolling hills northwest of the capital and major port of Cagliari. The varieties grown there — Cirò, Malvasia, Monica, Moscato, Nasco and Nuragus — carry the name of Cagliari in their denominations.

The northwestern coastal area around Sassari and Alghero and the wooded slopes of the Gallura peninsula in the northeast are noted for quality whites. Vermentino dominates the dry wines, though the non-DOC Torbato can be every bit as distinguished. Moscato is notable from Sorso and Sennori and Tempio Pausania. Vineyards in the rugged eastern coastal range around Nuoro are noted for the rich, red Cannonau.

Much of Sardinia's production is carried out by cooperatives. Among DOC wines, whites predominate by nearly two to one over reds. The most popular white variety is Nuragus, which is believed to have been brought there by the Phoenicians. Its name derives from the island's prehistoric stone towers known as *nuraghe*. Nuragus is the source of a modern dry white, clean and crisp if rather neutral in flavor.

Vermentino, a variety also planted in Liguria and parts of Tuscany, makes a white of distinct style in Sardinia, notably in the Gallura zone, though it can now be produced throughout the region as a light, often fizzy DOC wine.

The island's two important red varieties are Cannonau, a relative of the Granacha brought from Spain, and Monica, also of Spanish

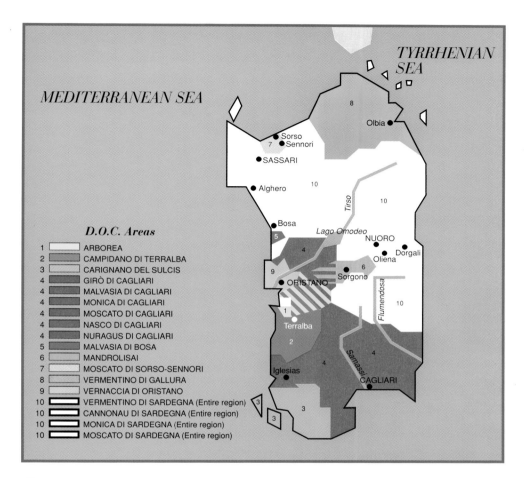

MEDITERRANEAN SEA

TYRRHENIAN SEA

D.O.C. Areas

1. ARBOREA
2. CAMPIDANO DI TERRALBA
3. CARIGNANO DEL SULCIS
4. GIRÒ DI CAGLIARI
4. MALVASIA DI CAGLIARI
4. MONICA DI CAGLIARI
4. MOSCATO DI CAGLIARI
4. NASCO DI CAGLIARI
4. NURAGUS DI CAGLIARI
5. MALVASIA DI BOSA
6. MANDROLISAI
7. MOSCATO DI SORSO-SENNORI
8. VERMENTINO DI GALLURA
9. VERNACCIA DI ORISTANO
10. VERMENTINO DI SARDEGNA (Entire region)
10. CANNONAU DI SARDEGNA (Entire region)
10. MONICA DI SARDEGNA (Entire region)
10. MOSCATO DI SARDEGNA (Entire region)

origin. Both can be dry or sweet, though trends favor the dry type toned down in strength from the traditionally heroic proportions. Cannonau of note comes from the towns of Oliena, Jerzu and Dorgali and the coastal hills of Capo Ferrato. It makes a fine sweet wine, which can be reminiscent of Port, as in the rich Anghelu Ruju. Carignano del Sulcis, from the southwest, is also of Spanish origin. A curiosity among the reds is the moderately sweet Girò di Cagliari.

Moscato can be either still or sparkling. Malvasia may be sweet, but is perhaps most impressive dry from the west coast town of Bosa and the Planargia hills.

The most distinctive of Sardinian wines is Vernaccia di Oristano. From a vine of uncertain origin grown in the flat, sandy Tirso river basin around Oristano, it becomes a Sherry-like amber wine with a rich array of nuances in bouquet and flavor.

23

Arborea	2 types: Sangiovese *R-P-Dr*; Trebbiano *W-Dr*, also *Sw, Fz*
Campidano di Terralba	*R-Dr*
Cannonau di Sardegna	*R-Dr*, also *Sw*, Ag-1, Rs Ag-3; Rosato *P-Dr*; Superiore Naturale *R-Dr*, also *Sw*, Ag-2; Liquoroso Dolce Naturale *R-Ft-Sw* or Secco *R-Ft-Dr*, Ag-1
Carignano del Sulcis	*R-Dr*, Rs Ag-2, also *P-Dr*
Girò di Cagliari	Dolce Naturale *R-Sw*; Secco *R-Dr*; Liquoroso *R-Ft-Sw/Dr*, Rs Ag-2
Malvasia di Bosa	*W-Dr/Sw*, also Liquoroso *W-Ft-Dr/Sw*, Ag-2
Malvasia di Cagliari	*W-Dr/Sw*, also Liquoroso *W-Ft-Dr/Sw*, Rs Ag-2
Mandrolisai	*R-P-Dr*, Sup Ag-2
Monica di Cagliari	*R-Sw/Dr*, also Liquoroso *R-Ft-Sw/Dr*, Rs Ag-2
Monica di Sardegna	*R-Dr*, Sup Ag-1
Moscato di Cagliari	*W-Sw*, also Liquoroso *W-Sw-Ft*, Rs Ag-1
Moscato di Sardegna	*W-Sw-Sp*
Moscato di Sorso-Sennori	*W-Sw*, also *Ft*
Nasco di Cagliari	*W-Sw/Dr*, also Liquoroso *W-Sw-Ft*, Rs Ag-2
Nuragus di Cagliari	*W-Dr*, also *Sw, Fz*
Vermentino di Gallura	*W-Dr*, also Sup
Vermentino di Sardegna	*W-Dr*, also *Sw, Sp*
Vernaccia di Oristano	*W-Dr*, also Liquoroso *W-Ft-Dr/Sw*, Ag-2, Sup Ag-3, Rs Ag-4

OTHER WINES OF NOTE

Red-Dry
Abbaìa
Cannonau di Alghero
Nebbiolo di Luras
Nièddera
Rosso di Berchidda
Tanca Farrà
Terre Brune
Turriga

White-Dry
Aragosta
Argiolas
Torbato di Alghero, also *Sp*
Vermentino di Usini

Others
Anghelu Ruju *R-Ft-Sw*
Malvasia di Planargia *W-Dr*, also *Ft, Sw*
Nasco di Ortueri *W-Sw/Dr*
Semidano di Mogoro *W-Dr/Sw*

Calabria

Regional capital: Catanzaro.

Provinces: Catanzaro, Cosenza, Reggio Calabria.

Calabria ranks 10th among the regions in size (15,080 square kilometers) and population (2,130,000).

Vineyards cover 31,600 hectares (10th) of which registered DOC plots total 3,400 hectares (15th).

Annual wine production of 1,100,000 hectoliters (14th) includes 3.6% or 40,000 hectoliters DOC (15th), of which about 90% is red.

*T*he toe of the Italian boot, Calabria is an overwhelmingly mountainous region with marked variations in microclimates between the warm coastal zones of the Ionian and Tyrrhenian seas and the chilly heights of the Sila and Aspromonte massifs. Two grape varieties of Greek origin dominate — Gaglioppo in red wines, Greco in whites — though the types of wine they make can vary markedly from one place to another.

Modern Oenotria's best-known wine is Cirò, which grows in low hills along the Ionian coast between the ancient Greek cities of Sybaris and Kroton (Sibari and Crotone today). Local legend has it that Cirò descended directly from Krimisa, the wine Calabrian athletes drank to celebrate victories in an early Olympiad.

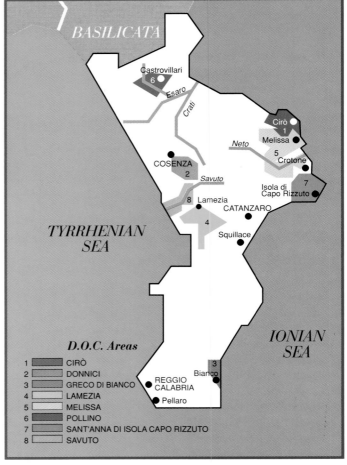

BASILICATA

Castrovillari
6
Esaro
Crati
Cirò
1
Melissa
Neto
5
COSENZA
2
Crotone
Savuto
Isola di
Capo Rizzuto
8 Lamezia
7
CATANZARO
4
TYRRHENIAN SEA
Squillace

IONIAN SEA

D.O.C. Areas

1	CIRÒ
2	DONNICI
3	GRECO DI BIANCO
4	LAMEZIA
5	MELISSA
6	POLLINO
7	SANT'ANNA DI ISOLA CAPO RIZZUTO
8	SAVUTO

3
Bianco
REGGIO
CALABRIA
Pellaro

   Lately Cirò has taken on contemporary touches as new methods of vine training and temperature-controlled winemaking have diminished the alcoholic strength (as well as the propensity to oxidize), making the wine rounder, fuller in fruit and fresher in bouquet. The classic Cirò is the *rosso*, which in *riserva* version has the capacity to age beyond a decade from certain vintages. There is also a *rosato* to drink young and a *bianco*, from Greco grapes, that can show impressively youthful freshness.

   Melissa, an adjacent DOC zone, has red and white wines similar to Cirò in content and style. But red wines from the same Gaglioppo grown at higher altitudes — Pollino, Donnici and Savuto, for example — are lighter in body and color, sometimes with fresh scents and flavors reminiscent of Alpine reds.

Among the whites, the rare Greco di Bianco stands out as one of the nation's finest sweet wines. From a local variety of Greco grown near the Ionian coast at the town of Bianco, it has a rich, velvety texture and an intriguing citrus-like bouquet. The nearly identical Greco di Gerace is a non-DOC wine that carries the ancient place name. From the same place comes Mantonico di Bianco, a Sherry-like amber wine with hints of almond and citrus in bouquet and flavor.

DOCs (8)

Cirò	*R-P-W-Dr*, RS (R) Ag-3
Donnici	*R-Dr*
Greco di Bianco	*W-Sw*, Ag-1
Lamezia	*R-Dr*
Melissa	*R-W-Dr*, Sup (R) Ag-2
Pollino	*R-Dr*, Sup Ag-2
Sant'Anna di Isola Capo Rizzuto	*R-P-Dr*
Savuto	*R-Dr*, Sup Ag-2

OTHER WINES OF NOTE

Red-Dry

Gravello

Lacrima di Castrovillari, also *P*

Pellaro

Ronco dei Quattro Venti

Others

Cerasuolo di Scilla, *P-Dr*

Greco di Gerace, *W-Sw*

Mantonico di Bianco, *W-Dr/Sw-Ft*

Moscato di Saracena, *W-Sw*

Valeo, *W-Sw*

Basilicata

Regional capital: Potenza.

Provinces: Matera, Potenza.

Basilicata ranks 14th in size among the regions (9,992 square kilometers) and 18th in population (619,000).

Vineyards cover 16,300 hectares (16th) of which registered DOC plots total 1,470 hectares (17th).

Annual wine production of 400,000 hectoliters (18th) includes 1.6% or 6,500 hectoliters DOC (18th), entirely red.

*B*asilicata, also known as Lucania, is an often neglected region of arid hills and desolate mountains that can be bitterly cold for a southerly place. But the cool upland climate has its advantages for viticulture, in wines that can show enviable aromas and flavors. Basilicata has only one DOC in Aglianico del Vulture, but that, at least, gives the inhabitants a source of pride. One of southern Italy's finest red wines, it is gradually gaining admirers elsewhere.

The Aglianico vine — which is also the base of Campania's vaunted Taurasi — was brought to Basilicata by the Greeks, perhaps as long ago as the 6th or 7th century BC. (Its name is a corruption of Hellenico). On the slopes of the extinct volcano known as Monte Vulture it makes a robust, deeply colored wine

that from fine vintages can improve for many years, becoming increasingly refined and complex in flavor. There are also youthful versions of the wine, sometimes semisweet and even sparkling, but the dry *vecchio* or *riserva*, after aging in oak casks, rates the most serious consideration.

Aglianico is also used for *vini da tavola* in other parts of the region, notably in the east around Matera, where reds from Sangiovese and Montepulciano also originate. White wines of interest are the sweet Moscato and Malvasia, the best of which come from the Vulture zone and the eastern Bradano valley.

DOCs (8)

Aglianico del Vulture	*R-Dr,* also *Sw,Sp,* Ag-1, Vecchio Ag-3, Rs Ag-5

OTHER WINES OF NOTE

Red-Dry

Aglianico dei Colli Lucani or di Matera, also *Sw, Sp*

Canneto

Metapontum

Montepulciano di Basilicata

White-Dry

Asprino or Asprinio, *Fz*

Metapontum

Others

Malvasia del Vulture, *W-Sw/Dr-Sp*

Malvasia della Lucania, *W-Dr/Sw-Sp*

Moscato del Vulture, *W-Sw-Sp*

Apulia (PUGLIA)

Regional capital: Bari.

Provinces: Bari, Brindisi, Foggia, Lecce, Taranto.

Apulia ranks 7th among the regions in size (19,347 square kilometers) and population (4,005,000).

Vineyards cover 132,000 hectares (2nd) of which registered DOC plots total 17,600 hectares (6th).

Annual wine production of 11,250,000 hectoliters (1st) includes 1.6% or 180,000 hectoliters DOC (12th), which takes in slightly more white than red and rosé.

*A*pulia, the heel of the Italian boot, is a long, relatively level region with a prolific production of both wine and table grapes. Its output of wine has surpassed Sicily's in most recent years as the most voluminous among the regions, a production that regularly surpasses that of Germany and all but six other nations. The title of "Europe's wine cellar" no longer carries much distinction. As markets for blending wines diminished, producers have tried to put the accent on premium wines.

Recently producers have come forth with some good to excellent bottlings of dry, balanced reds, whites and rosés from a range of grape varieties, both native and foreign. Apulia has 24 DOCs, by far the most of any southern region, yet, like its neighbors, it produces only a slight percentage of classified wine (1.6%). The region's remoteness and lack of clear-cut reputation for quality have inhibited commerce of wines in bottle.

Apulia can be divided roughly into two viticultural sectors by a hypothetical line crossing the region between Brindisi and Taranto. To the north the terrain is rolling to hilly and the climate is temperate, even cool at certain heights in the Murge plateau.

Dry wines from there tend to have moderate strength, with impressive fruit, good acidity and ample aroma. Red wines generally derive from the native Uva di Troia or Bombino Nero, as well as Montepulciano and Sangiovese. White wines are dominated by the Verdeca variety, though Bianco d'Alessano, Malvasia, Trebbiano and Bombino Bianco are also evident.

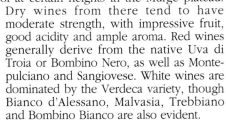

The leading DOC zone of northern Apulia is Castel del Monte, the one appellation that enjoys recognition abroad. It has a fine rosé and a full-bodied red that can be good young but often gains stature with age. In much of the

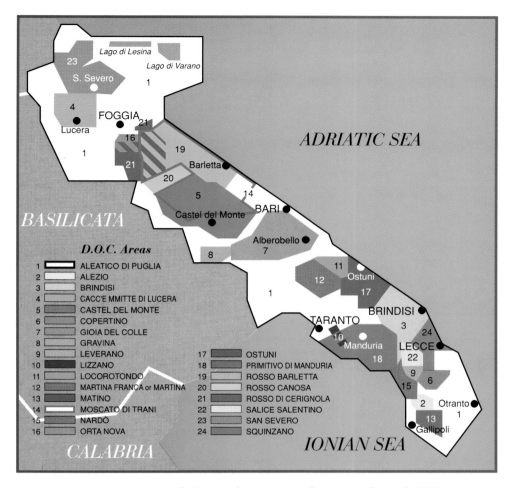

Lago di Lesina
Lago di Varano

23
S. Severo
1

4
FOGGIA
Lucera
21
16
1
19
21
20
Barletta
5
14
Castel del Monte
BARI
Alberobello
8
7
11
12
Ostuni
1
17
BRINDISI
TARANTO
3
10
24
Manduria
LECCE
18
22
9
6
15
2
Otranto
13
1
Gallipoli

ADRIATIC SEA

BASILICATA

CALABRIA

IONIAN SEA

D.O.C. Areas

1	ALEATICO DI PUGLIA
2	ALEZIO
3	BRINDISI
4	CACC'E MMITTE DI LUCERA
5	CASTEL DEL MONTE
6	COPERTINO
7	GIOIA DEL COLLE
8	GRAVINA
9	LEVERANO
10	LIZZANO
11	LOCOROTONDO
12	MARTINA FRANCA or MARTINA
13	MATINO
14	MOSCATO DI TRANI
15	NARDÒ
16	ORTA NOVA
17	OSTUNI
18	PRIMITIVO DI MANDURIA
19	ROSSO BARLETTA
20	ROSSO CANOSA
21	ROSSO DI CERIGNOLA
22	SALICE SALENTINO
23	SAN SEVERO
24	SQUINZANO

north the emphasis is on red wines under such DOCs as Rosso Canosa, Rosso Barletta and Rosso di Cerignola.

Just north of the Brindisi-Taranto line white wines dominate, in particular those of the Itria valley — Locorotondo and Martina Franca. Throughout the region experimentation is under way with outside varieties: Chardonnay, Pinot Bianco and Sauvignon among the whites; Cabernet, Malbec and Pinot Nero among the reds.

South of the Brindisi-Taranto line lies Salento, a flat peninsula that extends toward Albania and Greece as Italy's easternmost point. Though hot, it is not quite torrid, thanks to the play of breezes off the Adriatic and Ionian seas. Salento's traditional wines were the powerful, inky reds from Primitivo, Negroamaro and Malvasia Nera, but increasing attention is being given to lighter reds and rosés, as well as some surprisingly fresh and fruity whites.

Primitivo di Manduria, the early ripening grape that had made a favored blending wine, is apparently related to California's Zinfandel. Differences in vine training and methods and purposes of winemaking between Salento and California have resulted in distinct style variations, yet a family resemblance can be noted in the heavy and somewhat wild aspects of the wines.

Among the many DOCs of Salento, Salice Salentino stands out for its rich red and rosé, though such obscure appellations as Squinzano, Brindisi, Alezio and Copertino can show unexpected class. Salento's *vini da tavola* can also be intriguing, under such individual names as Notarpanaro, Portulano, Cappello di Prete and some rosés that rank with Italy's finest.

Aleatico di Puglia	R-Sw-Ft, Rs Ag-3
Alezio	R-P-Dr, Rs (R) Ag-2
Brindisi	R-P-Dr, Rs (R) Ag-2
Cacc'e mmitte di Lucera	R-Dr
Castel del Monte	R-P-W-Dr, Rs (R) Ag-3
Copertino	R-P-Dr, Rs (R) Ag-2
Gioia del Colle	5 types: Aleatico R-Sw-Ft, Rs Ag-2; Bianco W-Dr; Primitivo R-Dr, also Sw, Rs Ag-2; Rosato P-Dr; Rosso R-Dr
Gravina	W-Dr, also Sw, Sp
Leverano	R-P-W-Dr, also (W) Sp, Rs (R) Ag-2
Lizzano	5 types: Bianco W-Dr, also Fz, Sp; Rosato P-Dr, also Sp; Rosso R-Dr, also Fz, Novello; Malvasia Nera R-Dr, Sup Ag-1; Negro Amaro R-P-Dr, Sup (R) Ag-1
Locorotondo	W-Dr, also Sp
Martina Franca or Martina	W-Dr, also Sp
Matino	R-P-Dr
Moscato di Trani	W-Sw, also Liquoroso W-Sw-Ft, Ag-1
Nardò	R-P-Dr, Rs (R) Ag-2
Orta Nova	R-P-Dr
Ostuni	2 types: Bianco W-Dr, Ottavianello R-Dr
Primitivo di Manduria	R-Dr/Sw, also Liquoroso R-Dr/Sw-Ft, Ag-2
Rosso Barletta	R-Dr, Invecchiato Ag-2
Rosso Canosa	R-Dr, Rs Ag-2
Rosso di Cerignola	R-Dr, Rs Ag-2
Salice Salentino	6 types: Rosso R-Dr, also Novello, Rs Ag-2; Rosato P-Dr, also Sp; Bianco W-Dr; Aleatico R-Sw, also Ft, Rs Ag-2; Pinot Bianco W-Dr also Sp; Liquoroso W-Sw
San Severo	R-P-W-Dr, also (W) Sp
Squinzano	R-P-Dr, Rs (R) Ag-2

OTHER WINES OF NOTE

Red-Dry	*White-Dry*	*Others*
Cabernet di Puglia	Bianco del Salento	Five Roses, P-Dr
Cappello di Prete	Bolina	Negrino, R-Sw
Donna Marzia	Chardonnay del Salento	Rosa del Golfo, P-Dr
Duca d'Aragona	Cantico	Rosato del Salento, P-Dr
Graticciaia	Chardonnay di Puglia	
Notarpanaro	Le Viscarde	
Portulano	Pinot Bianco di Puglia	
Quarantale	Preludio No.1	
Rosso di Salento	Sauvignon di Puglia	
Vigna Spano	Verdeca del Salento	

Campania

Regional capital: Naples (Napoli).

Provinces: Avellino, Benevento, Caserta, Napoli, Salerno.

Campania ranks 12th among the regions in size (13,595 square kilometers) and 2nd in population (5,650,000).

Vineyards cover 46,800 hectares (9th) of which registered DOC plots total 1,550 hectares (16th).

Annual wine production of 2,500,000 hectoliters (9th) includes 1% or 25,000 hectoliters DOC (16th), about two-thirds of which is white.

*T*he ancient Romans considered Campania Felix to be the *ne plus ultra* of wine regions. They favored the vineyards along the coast north of Naples where Falernum, the most treasured wine of the empire, was grown. They also lauded the wines of Vesuvius and the hills of Avellino. The Greeks, too, recognized the privileged nature of the place, introducing vines which still stand out today in Aglianico and Greco.

Campania's vinicultural fortunes had been declining for decades as growers left the land and a majority of producers ignored DOC. But there have always been exceptions, none more conspicuous than the trio of classified wines—the red Taurasi and the white Fiano di Avellino and Greco di Tufo—all grown in the hills east of Naples.

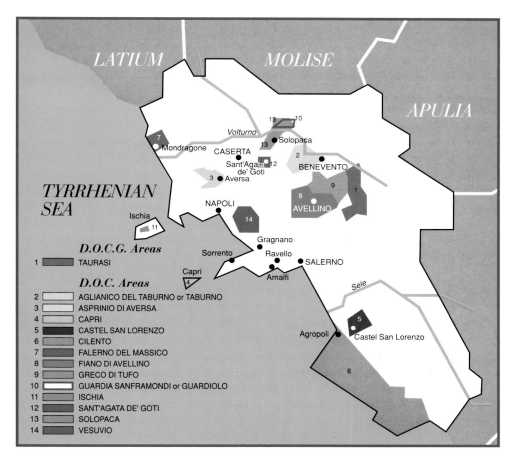

LATIUM

MOLISE

APULIA

TYRRHENIAN
SEA

Volturno
7 Mondragone
CASERTA
Sant'Agata
de' Goti
3 Aversa

13 10
Solopaca
13
12
2
BENEVENTO
9
8
AVELLINO
1

Ischia
11

NAPOLI
14

D.O.C.G. Areas

1   TAURASI

D.O.C. Areas

2   AGLIANICO DEL TABURNO or TABURNO
3   ASPRINIO DI AVERSA
4   CAPRI
5   CASTEL SAN LORENZO
6   CILENTO
7   FALERNO DEL MASSICO
8   FIANO DI AVELLINO
9   GRECO DI TUFO
10 GUARDIA SANFRAMONDI or GUARDIOLO
11 ISCHIA
12 SANT'AGATA DE' GOTI
13 SOLOPACA
14 VESUVIO

Gragnano
Sorrento
Ravello
Capri
Amalfi
SALERNO
Sele
5
Agropoli
Castel San Lorenzo
6

Taurasi, from Aglianico, has been called "the Barolo of the south" due to its size and ability to age, though its style is proudly its own. That red wine has been promoted to DOCG. Fiano and Greco are among Italy's most distinguished whites. Credit for their status is due largely to the Mastroberardino winery which has carried these historically significant but once nearly forgotten vines to new heights of prestige.

The wines of Ischia and Solopaca rate increasing praise, as does the DOC of Falerno del Massico, where the ancient Falernum was grown. Recently the region's wine authorities have put the emphasis on controlled quality in new zones designed to revive Campania's historical potential.

DOCGs (1)

Taurasi	R-Dr, Ag-3, Rs Ag-4

DOCs (13)

Aglianico del Taburno or Taburno	R-Dr Ag-1, Rs Ag-3
Asprinio di Aversa	W-Dr, also Sp
Capri	R-W-Dr
Castel San Lorenzo	6 types: Bianco W-Dr; Barbera R-Dr, Rs Ag-2; Rosso R-Dr; Rosato P-Dr; Moscato W-Sw; Moscato Spumante W-Sw-Sp
Cilento	4 types: Rosso R-Dr, Rosato P-Dr, Bianco W-Dr, Aglianico R-Dr, Ag-1
Falerno del Massico	3 types: Rosso R-Dr, Ag-1, Rs Ag-2; Bianco W-Dr, Primitivo R-Dr, Ag-1
Fiano di Avellino	W-Dr
Greco di Tufo	W-Dr
Guardia Sanframondi or Guardiolo	6 types: Bianco W-Dr; Falanghina W-Dr; Spumante W-Dr-Sp; Aglianico R-Dr, Rs Ag-2; Rosso R-Dr, also Novello, Rs Ag-2; Rosato P-Dr
Ischia	R-W-Dr, also (W) Sp
Sant'Agata de' Goti	7 types: Bianco W-Dr; Falanghina W-Dr, also Passito W-Sw; Greco W-Dr; Aglianico R-Dr, Ag-2, Rs Ag-3; Piedirosso R-Dr, Rs Ag-2; Rosso R-Dr, also Novello, Rs Ag-2; Rosato P-Dr
Solopaca	R-W-Dr
Vesuvio	R-P-W-Dr; Lacryma Christi del Vesuvio R-P-W-Dr, also Sp, Liquoroso W-Ft-Sw/Dr

OTHER WINES OF NOTE

Red-Dry

Aglianico del Sannio
Barbera
Gragnano, also Fz/Sp, Sw
Lettere, also Fz
Per'e Palummo
Ravello

White-Dry

Biancolella
Falanghina
Forastera
Plinius
Ravello

Others

Kalimera, W-Sp
Lacrimarosa, P-Dr
Ravello, P-Dr

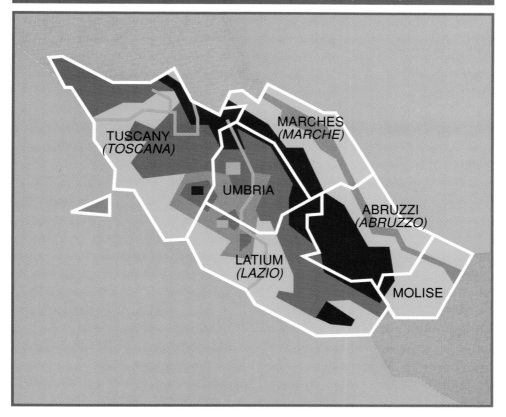

*T*he historical hills at the heart of the peninsula, favored by ample sunshine and moderate temperatures, boast what seem to be the nation's most extensive natural conditions for fine wine. In the past winemaking methods were often rustic. The practices of overproducing grapes and under-valuing scientific techniques too often squandered the excellent potential. But today the central regions, led by Tuscany with Chianti and other noble reds, are rapidly moving to the forefront of Italian enology.

Between them, the six regions produce less than a quarter of the nation's wine, yet they account for about a third of the DOC or DOCG. The conflict between progress and tradition persists in places, but overall the renaissance in Italian wine has generated unrivalled momentum in the heartland. There is no doubt that greater things lie ahead. The regions of central Italy are divided physically, and to some degree culturally, by the Apennines. To the west, on the Tyrrhenian side, lie Tuscany, Latium and landlocked Umbria. To the east, on the Adriatic side, lie the Marches, Abruzzi and Molise. Viticulture on the Tyrrhenian side is dominated by the dark-skinned Sangiovese (whose various clones include some of Italy's noblest grapes for red wine) and the light-skinned Trebbiano and Malvasia (designed chiefly for quantities of tasty if rarely inspiring whites).

The realm of Sangiovese is Florence's region of Tuscany, where it prevails in Chianti — the nation's archetypal wine — as well as in Brunello di Montalcino, Vino Nobile di Montepulciano and most of the noteworthy classified and unclassified reds. White Malvasia reigns in Rome's region of Latium. It is prominent in Frascati and the wines of the Alban hills, and combines with the ubiquitous Trebbiano in Est! Est!! Est!!! and most other whites of the region. Umbrians have had the chance to pick and choose, favoring Sangiovese for their reds and the Procanico strain of Trebbiano for their prominent white Orvieto.

The trend, though perhaps more evident in Tuscany and Umbria than elsewhere, is to introduce noble outsiders —

Cabernet Sauvignon, Merlot, the Pinots, Chardonnay and Sauvignon. But efforts are also being directed at upgrading such worthy natives as Vernaccia di San Gimignano, Umbria's Sagrantino and Grechetto and Latium's Cesanese.

The Adriatic regions have a rather neat and straight-forward structure of vines and wines. Vineyards are almost all planted in hills running in a tortuous strip between the sea and the mountains, where the climate is tempered by cool air currents.

Two native varieties stand out along the Adriatic coast, the white Verdicchio in the Marches and red Montepulciano, which originated in the Abruzzi and is now widely planted in all three regions. The influences of Tuscany and Romagna can be tasted in Sangiovese (especially in the Marches) and Trebbiano (planted nearly everywhere that worthier varieties are not). Montepulciano can be remarkable on its own, though it also has a natural affinity for blends with Sangiovese, in such fine reds as the Marches' Rosso Piceno and Rosso Conero.

Regional and national capital: Rome (Roma).

Provinces: Frosinone, Latina, Rieti, Roma, Viterbo.

Latium ranks 9th among the regions in size (17,203 square kilometers) and 3rd in population (5,102,000).

Vineyards cover 65,500 hectares (8th) of which registered DOC plots total 17,400 hectares (7th).

Annual wine production of 5,000,000 hectoliters (5th) includes 11% or 535,000 hectoliters DOC (6th), of which about 95% is white.

*R*ome's region is intrinsically linked to white wine — to Frascati and Marino and the other golden-hued *bianchi* of the Castelli Romani and to the fabled Est! Est!! Est!!! from the northern Latium town of Montefiascone. These wines, which are based almost esclusively on various types of Malvasia and Trebbiano, were traditionally *abboccato*, mouth filling, though not so sweet as to overwhelm the flavor of food. They were easy, everyday wines not designed to last long or travel far.

The introduction of low temperaure processing and sterile filtration have transformed their personalities into dryer, crisper, lighter, more durable wines with a propensity to travel that has opened up new commercial horizons. Still, with only the occasional exception, the whites of Latium are pleasantly fleshy and fruity, wines that go enticingly well with a great range of foods but are not the sort to be laid away or fussed over.

Their immediacy is by no means a negative attribute, as evidenced by the established world market for Frascati (which ranks in the top ten DOCs in volume with nearly 20 millon liters a year). Marino and less publicized but worthy neighbors in Colli Albani, Colli Lanuvini and Montecompatri-Colonna. Though some admirers argue that the fuller, stronger *abboccato* or *cannellino* versions are what Malvasia is all about, the world's consumers seem to prefer them softly dry.

The ancient Romans drank white wines, too, though Horace and company reserved their greatest praise for the red Falernum and Caecubum - which were grown along the southern coast near Gaeta and Sperlonga. Even today, though white wine accounts for an overwhelming share of the region's production, certain of Latium's red wines seem to be more convincing to connoisseurs.

The DOC reds vary in composition. Aprilia, in the reclaimed stretches of what were once the Pontine Marshes, turns out considerable quantities of Merlot and Sangiovese. The reds of Cerveteri, Cori and Velletri are based on Montepulciano and Sangiovese. The native Cesanese makes richly flavored dry and

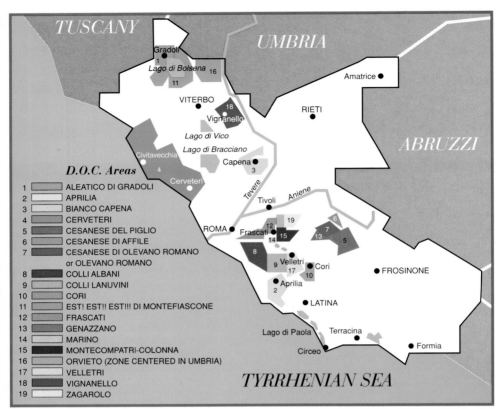

D.O.C. Areas

1. ALEATICO DI GRADOLI
2. APRILIA
3. BIANCO CAPENA
4. CERVETERI
5. CESANESE DEL PIGLIO
6. CESANESE DI AFFILE
7. CESANESE DI OLEVANO ROMANO or OLEVANO ROMANO
8. COLLI ALBANI
9. COLLI LANUVINI
10. CORI
11. EST! EST!! EST!!! DI MONTEFIASCONE
12. FRASCATI
13. GENAZZANO
14. MARINO
15. MONTECOMPATRI-COLONNA
16. ORVIETO (ZONE CENTERED IN UMBRIA)
17. VELLETRI
18. VIGNANELLO
19. ZAGAROLO

Map labels: TUSCANY, UMBRIA, ABRUZZI, Gradoli, Lago di Bolsena, Amatrice, VITERBO, Vignanello, RIETI, Lago di Vico, Lago di Bracciano, Civitavecchia, Capena, Cerveteri, Tevere, Tivoli, Aniene, ROMA, Frascati, FROSINONE, Velletri, Cori, Aprilia, LATINA, Lago di Paola, Terracina, Formia, Circeo, TYRRHENIAN SEA

sweet reds in the three DOC zones of the Prenestina and Ciociaria hills southeast of Rome. Aleatico makes a Port-like dessert wine on the northern shores of Lake Bolsena at Gradoli.

Cabernet and Merlot are the stars in three highly praised modern *vini da tavola* of Latium, in Fiorano Rosso and Colle Picchioni from just south of Rome and in Torre Ercolana, which combines the French varieties with Cesanese, at the hill town of Anagni. Latium's modern Falernum is based on Aglianico and Caecubum, now called Cecubo, is made up of the local Abbuoto with some Negroamaro. These reds, and others, prove that fortunes of premium wine production in Latium are not entirely white.

DOCs (18)*

Aleatico di Gradoli	*R-Sw*, also *Ft*
Aprilia	3 types: Merlot *R-Dr*; Sangiovese *R-P-Dr*; Trebbiano *W-Dr*
Bianco Capena	*W-Dr*, also *Sw*

Cerveteri	*R-W-Dr*
Cesanese del Piglio	*R-Dr*, also *Sw, Fz, Sp*
Cesanese di Affile	*R-Dr*, also *Sw, Fz, Sp*
Cesanese di Olevano Romano	*R-Dr*, also *Sw, Fz, Sp*
Colli Albani	*W-Dr*, also *Sw, Sp*
Colli Lanuvini	*W-Dr*, also *Sw*
Cori	*R-W-Dr*, also (W) *Sw*
Est! Est!! Est!!! di Montefiascone	*W-Dr*, also *Sw*
Frascati	*W-Dr*, also *Sw, Sp, Novello*
Genazzano	*R-W-Dr*, also *Novello*
Marino	*W-Dr*, also *Sw, Sp*
Montecompatri-Colonna	*W-Dr*, also *Sw*
Velletri	*R-Dr*, also *Sw*, Rs Ag-2; *W-Dr*, also *Sw, Sp*
Vignanello	5 types: Bianco *W-Dr*; Greco *W-Dr*; Greco Spumante *W-Dr-Sp*; Rosso *R-Dr*, also *Novello*, Rs Ag-2; Rosato *P-Dr*
Zagarolo	*W-Dr*, also *Sw*
* Note: the Orvieto DOC zone centered in Umbria also extends into Latium	

OTHER WINES OF NOTE

Red-Dry	White-Dry	Others
Castelli Romani	Castelli Romani	Albiola, *P-Dr*
Cecubo	Fiorano Bianco	Cardellino, *P-Dr*
Colle Picchioni	Rigogolo	Castelli Romani, *P-Dr*
Falernum	Satrico	Fiorano Sémillon, *W-Sw*
Fiorano Rosso		Moscato di Terracina, *W-Sw*
Maccarese		
Madreselva		
Nibbio		
Santa Giulia		
Torre Ercolana		

Molise

Regional capital: Campobasso.

Provinces: Campobasso, Isernia.

Molise ranks 19th among the regions in size (4,438 square kilometers) and in population (334,000).

Vineyards cover 9,350 hectares (18th) of which registered DOC plots total 157 hectares (19th).

Annual wine production of 550,000 hectoliters (19th) includes 0.36% or 2,000 hectoliters DOC (20th), of which about 80% is red.

*T*his overlooked region, which was long an appendix of the Abruzzi, gained official status in wine in the 1980s with the DOCs of Biferno and Pentro. The undeniable aptitude for vines on the sunny hillsides between the Apennines and the Adriatic indicates that Molise's wines could match those of neighboring Abruzzi, Apulia or Campania with time, though the evidence in bottle is scarce so far. The soil in the region's hills and the mild Adriatic climate seem to provide a favorable combination.

The estates of Masseria Di Majo Norante with DOC of Biferno and the table wines of Ramitello are setting examples for others to follow as Molise strives for a vinicultural identity of its own. Most other wine seems to be consumed locally, which explains why Molise has the smallest percentage of classified wines in its total.

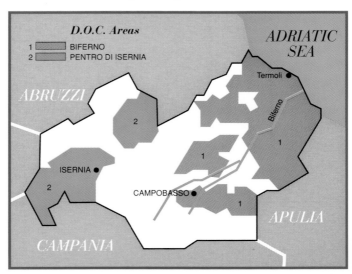

D.O.C. Areas
1 BIFERNO
2 PENTRO DI ISERNIA

ADRIATIC SEA

ABRUZZI

Termoli

Biferno

ISERNIA

CAMPOBASSO

APULIA

CAMPANIA

| **Biferno** | R-P-W-Dr, Rs (R) Ag-3 |
| **Pentro di Isernia** | R-P-W-Dr |

OTHER WINES OF NOTE

Red-Dry	**White-Dry**	**Others**
Aglianico	Bianco del Molise	Rosato del Molise
Montepulciano	Malvasia	Moscato, W-Sw
Ramitello Rosso	Ramitello Bianco	
Rosso del Molise	Trebbiano	
Sangiovese		

Abruzzi (ABRUZZO)

Regional capital: L'Aquila.

Provinces: Chieti, L'Aquila, Pescara, Teramo.

Abruzzi ranks 14th among the regions in size (10,749 square kilometers) and in population (1,250,000).

Vineyards cover 30,000 hectares (13th) of which registered DOC plots total 9,800 hectares (12th).

Annual wine production of 3,800,000 hectoliters (6th) includes 8.5% or 320,000 hectoliters DOC (9th), of which about 65% is red.

*I*n a nation of myriad appellations, the Abruzzi offers wine drinkers rare and refreshing simplicity. There are only two DOCs and precious few unclassified wines of note in a region that is two-thirds mountains and one-third hills with highly favorable natural conditions for grapevines. Growers favor the predominant Montepulciano and Trebbiano, source of their two regional DOCs, while growing some highly productive vines (the region has Italy's highest average yields) for table wine and table grapes and experimenting in a so far unconvincing way with outside varieties.

Still, despite the outward simplicity, certain nuances of production are worth pointing out. The native Montepulciano (not to be confused with the town of that name in Tuscany where Vino Nobile is made) is a vine of undeniable distinction, even if its inherent class is not as widely acclaimed as it deserves to be. In parts of the Abruzzi, most notably in the low hills of the northern province of Teramo, Montepulciano becomes a red of irresistible character — full-bodied, even robust, with a capacity to age but with such supple smoothness that it can be eminently drinkable even when young. In higher inland areas, or from vineyards where growers have the habit of excessive yields, the wines tend to be lighter, often better suited to Cerasuolo, a sturdy, cherry-colored rosé. A fair quantity of inky, strong blending wine is also produced in the region.

Most Trebbiano is based on the prolific Tuscan variety, which makes light, rather acidic whites of subtle aroma and flavor. A few growers work with the "true" Trebbiano d'Abruzzo (which may or may not be related to the Bombino Bianco of Apulia). One manages to make a Trebbiano of remarkable depth and texture, with a propensity to develop almost Burgundy-like complexity with four or five years, sometimes even more, of aging. But these fine wines are rarely found in commerce, even in Italy.

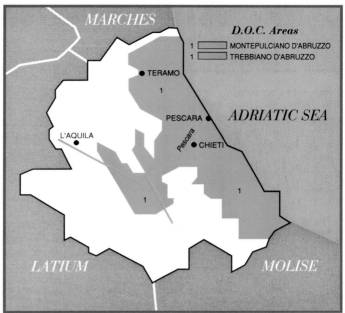

D.O.C. Areas

| 1 | MONTEPULCIANO D'ABRUZZO |
| 1 | TREBBIANO D'ABRUZZO |

MARCHES

TERAMO

PESCARA

ADRIATIC SEA

L'AQUILA

CHIETI

LATIUM

MOLISE

DOCs (2)

| Montepulciano d'Abruzzo | R-Dr, Rs Ag-2; Cerasuolo P-Dr |
| Trebbiano d'Abruzzo | W-Dr, also Fz |

OTHER WINES OF NOTE

Red-Dry
Abbazia di Propezzano
Angelo Rosso
Capsico
Leneo Moro

White-Dry
Angelo Bianco
Ciafré

Others
Moscato, W-Sw

Marches (MARCHE)

Regional capital: Ancona.

Provinces: Ancona, Ascoli Piceno, Macerata, Pesaro, Urbino.

The Marches ranks 15th among the regions in size (9,694 square kilometers) and 13th in population (1,426,000).

Vineyards cover 31,000 hectares (11th) of which registered DOC plots total 10,000 hectares (11th).

Annual wine production of 2,100,000 hectoliters (10th) includes 13% or 282,000 hectoliters DOC (10th), of which about 75% is white.

Verdicchio is plenipotentiary for the wines of this pleasant Adriatic region, whose devotion to whites should not obscure the worthiness of its reds. The Castelli di Jesi DOC zone, covering a vast tract of hills west of the port of Ancona, is the home of the Verdicchio that made an early impression abroad in its green amphora bottles.

But recently producers have created a new image of Verdicchio as a white of special character that comes across even more convincingly in standard bottles. Quality has risen so steadily that even wine still sold in amphora seems a cut above the general level of popular whites. This seems to herald a revival for a white produced at the rate of more than 20 million bottles a year that has been described as Italy's premier wine to serve with fish.

Verdicchio di Matelica, grown in limited quantities in a higher inland zone, can have more body and strength. From some estates it can develop into a white of unexpected depth and character after two or three years in bottle. Verdicchio from both DOC zones and elsewhere makes convincing sparkling wine as well, usually by the charmat method, but also occasionally by the classical method of bottle fermentation. Until two decades ago, when Verdicchio was still largely a local wine, it was more often bubbly than not.

The region's other white wines, such as Bianchello del Metauro and Falerio dei Colli Ascolani, are usually light and zesty, also invariably good with seafood.

The red wines of the Marches are based chiefly on Sangiovese or Montepulciano — sometimes blended, sometimes not. The most important, in terms of volume, is Rosso Piceno, dominated by Sangiovese. It comes from a DOC zone covering nearly the entire eastern flank of the region stretching from the Superiore area between Ascoli Piceno and the sea north through the coastal hills to Senigallia.

Rosso Conero, dominated by Montepulciano, originates in a small zone on the slopes of the Conero massif south of Ancona.

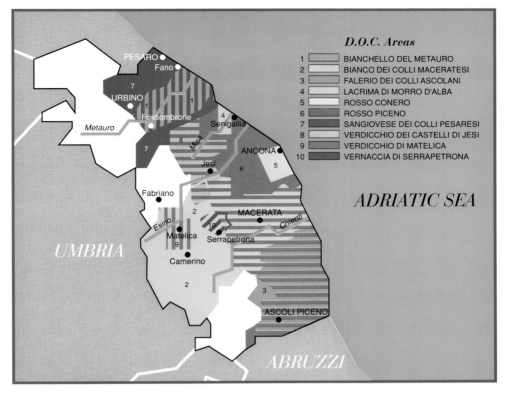

D.O.C. Areas

1	BIANCHELLO DEL METAURO
2	BIANCO DEI COLLI MACERATESI
3	FALERIO DEI COLLI ASCOLANI
4	LACRIMA DI MORRO D'ALBA
5	ROSSO CONERO
6	ROSSO PICENO
7	SANGIOVESE DEI COLLI PESARESI
8	VERDICCHIO DEI CASTELLI DI JESI
9	VERDICCHIO DI MATELICA
10	VERNACCIA DI SERRAPETRONA

Both wines are habitually made to drink within two to four years, when they are persuasively round and fresh in flavor, though certain producers have made wines that age remarkably well from good vintages — sometimes for a decade or more. The DOC Sangiovese dei Colli Pesaresi, from the northern Marches, bears a strong family resemblance to the Sangiovese of neighboring Romagna.

DOCs (10)

Bianchello del Metauro	W-Dr
Bianco dei Colli Maceratesi	W-Dr
Falerio dei Colli Ascolani	W-Dr
Lacrima di Morro	R-Dr, also *Sw, Sp*
Rosso Conero	R-Dr, Rs Ag-2
Rosso Piceno	R-Dr, Sup Ag-1

Sangiovese dei Colli Pesaresi	*R-Dr*
Verdicchio dei Castelli di Jesi	*W-Dr,* also *Sp*
Verdicchio di Matelica	*W-Dr,* also *Sp*
Vernaccia di Serrapetrona	*R-Dr/Sw-Sp*

OTHER WINES OF NOTE

Red-Dry	Vernaculum	Verdicchio Pian delle Mura
Braccano		
Montepulciano delle Marche	*White-Dry*	*Others*
Rosso di Corinaldo	Antico di Casa Fosca	Donna Giulia, P-Dr-Sp
Rozzano	Le Busche	Kòmaros, P-Dr
Tenuta di Pongelli	Le Moie	Rosato di Montanello, P-Dr
Vellutato	Monsanulus	Vin Santo, W-Sw
Vernaccia di Pergola	Verdicchio di Montanello	

Umbria

Regional capital: Perugia.

Provinces: Perugia, Terni.

Umbria ranks 16th among the regions in size (8,456 square kilometers) and 17th in population (817,000).

Vineyards cover 22,000 hectares (14th) of which registered DOC plots total 5,600 hectares (14th).

Annual wine production of 1,100,000 hectoliters (16th) includes 15% or 165,000 hectoliters DOC or DOCG (13th), of which more than 80% is white.

*U*mbria has long been renowned for white wine, thanks mainly to the historical prominence of Orvieto. But evidence grows that the hills of the "green heart of Italy" have an aptitude for a multitude of varieties, white and red, native and foreign.

Orvieto was once the most celebrated of Italian whites as a semisweet or *abboccato* wine, praised by the popes, princes and painters who sojourned in the hill town north of Rome with its splendid Cathedral and sweeping views of the Umbrian landscape. But as tastes changed Orvieto has been modified from a soft, golden wine into a pale, pure, crisp creature of the technology of soft-crushed grapes and free-run musts processed at low temperatures.

Some laud the change, others deplore it as a travesty of tradition. But modern Orvieto is a commercial success as one of Italy's best-selling DOC whites with a solid following abroad. Actually, some producers are turning back a bit, in a sense, striving for more character in the wine through lower grape yields and more meticulous selection and by letting the grapeskins remain in contact with the juice for a while before fermentation. Just lately Orvieto's *abboccato* has made a comeback as a dessert wine. Though Procanico (Trebbiano) and Malvasia prevail in Orvieto, growers in the zone have been working successfully with such outside varieties as Chardonnay, Sauvignon, the Pinots and Gewürztraminer, as well as the admirable local Grechetto.

But the most prestigious Umbrian wine is the red Torgiano Rosso *riserva*, which has been given special status as DOCG (though the regular Torgiano red and white remain DOC). A modern classic based on Sangiovese, the *riserva*, under the name Rubesco, has been known to age to unique splendor for a decade or two. Sagrantino, a vine grown around the hill town of Montefalco, is an intriguing native that yields both dry and sweet wines of unmistakable grandeur. It has been selected for a special DOCG. Among the many outside varieties planted in Umbria,

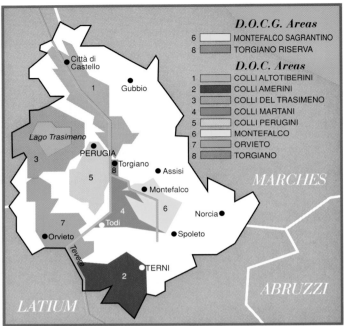

D.O.C.G. Areas
6 MONTEFALCO SAGRANTINO
8 TORGIANO RISERVA

D.O.C. Areas
1 COLLI ALTOTIBERINI
2 COLLI AMERINI
3 COLLI DEL TRASIMENO
4 COLLI MARTANI
5 COLLI PERUGINI
6 MONTEFALCO
7 ORVIETO
8 TORGIANO

Merlot and Barbera have been prominent for more than a century. More recently, Cabernet Sauvignon has shown promise, both as a varietal wine and in blends. Even Pinot Nero has given indications of more than the usual class here.

Umbria has numerous curiosities among its vines and wines, though few of the local rarities ever leave the region. Vin Santo, pressed from semidried Grechetto or Malvasia grapes, is usually sweet and most prized by Umbrians as a wine for any occasion.

DOCGs (2)

*Montefalco Sagrantino**	*R-Dr* or Passito *R-SW*, Ag-3
*Torgiano Rosso Riserva**	*R-Dr*, Ag-3

DOCs (8)

Colli Altotiberini	*R-P-W-Dr*
Colli Amerini	4 types: Novello *R-Dr*, also Sup; *P-Dr; W-Dr;* Malvasia *W-Dr*
Colli del Trasimeno	*R-W-Dr*
Colli Martani	3 types: Grechetto (also Grechetto di Todi) *W-Dr;* Sangiovese *R-Dr*, Ag-1, Rs Ag-2; Trebbiano *W-Dr*
Colli Perugini	*R-P-W-Dr*
*Montefalco**	Rosso *R-Dr*, Rs Ag-3; Bianco *W-Dr*

Orvieto	*W-Dr*, also *Sw*
*Torgiano**	9 types: Bianco *W-Dr;* Rosso *R-Dr;* Rosato *P-Dr;* Cabernet Sauvignon *R-Dr,* Ag-1; Chardonnay *W-Dr;* Pinot Grigio *W-Dr;* Pinot Nero *R-Dr,* Ag-1; Riesling Italico *W-Dr;* Spumante *W-Dr-Sp*

*The DOCG denominations are only for Montefalco Sagrantino and Torgiano Rosso Riserva. The other wines of Montefalco and Torgiano are DOC, though they cover the same zones.

OTHER WINES OF NOTE

Red-Dry	White-Dry	Others
Cabernet Sauvignon	Bianco d'Arquata	Calcaia, W-Sw
Casole Rosso	Bianco di Assisi	Castel Grifone, P-Dr
Foresco	Borro della Sala	Decugnano Brut, W-Sp
Lago di Corbara	Casole Bianco	Lungarotti Brut, W-Sp
Merlot di Spello	Cervaro della Sala	Muffa Nobile, W-Sw
Monrubio	Chardonnay di Miralduolo	Pourriture Noble, W-Sw
Pinot Nero	Grecante	Solleone, W-Ft-Dr
Rosso d'Arquata	Grechetto di Umbria	
Rosso di Assisi	Marrano	
San Giorgio	Pomaio	

Tuscany *(TOSCANA)*

Regional capital: Florence (Firenze).

Provinces: Arezzo, Firenze, Grosseto, Livorno, Lucca, Massa-Carrara, Pisa, Pistoia, Siena.

Tuscany ranks 5th among the regions in size (22,992 square kilometers) and 9th in population (3,577,000).

Vineyards cover 86,000 hectares (4th) of which registered DOC plots total 30,500 hectares (3rd).

Annual wine production of 3,600,000 hectoliters (8th) includes 33% or 1,200,000 hectoliters DOC or DOCG (tied for 2nd with Piedmont), of which more than 85% is red.

*F*lorence's region has shifted its stance in the last couple of decades from a complacent supplier of flask Chianti to the nation's most creative producer of premium wines. Tuscany's revolution began in Chianti and the central hills around Siena but quickly spread to take in the coastal zones that were not previously noted for vineyards.

Much of the progress has come with classical reds — Brunello di Montalcino, Vino Nobile di Montepulciano, Chianti and Carmignano — all DOCG. But growing success with other reds (including the stylish table wines sometimes called "Super Tuscans") has been augmented by a new breed of whites to enhance the region's reputation. Vernaccia di San Gimignano's promotion to DOCG gave Tuscany five of the nation's thirteen guaranteed wines.

Chianti, still the dominant force in Tuscan viniculture, has ranked as the most Italian of wines for decades. This is partly because it is the most voluminous and widely sold classified wine, but also because it has a personality that cannot be pinned down; in its enigmatic way it is unequivocally Italian. Chianti can be light, easy, quaffable on the one hand, dignified, elaborate, austere on the other. It is produced in seven distinct subzones, including the original core area of Chianti Classico, that cover a vast territory of central Tuscany. In these often rugged hills variations in soil and climate contribute as much to the individuality of each authentic estate wine as do producers' quests for a personal style. These variations may be confusing, but for consumers who persist Chianti offers some of the best quality for value in wine today.

Since Chianti was elevated to DOCG in 1984, its production has sharply diminished and its quality has markedly improved. Chianti may be identified by its subdistricts, though only producers of Classico — whose consortium is symbolized by a black rooster — have made much of a geographical point so far. Many estates emphasize the name of a certain vineyard or area as a mark of distinction.

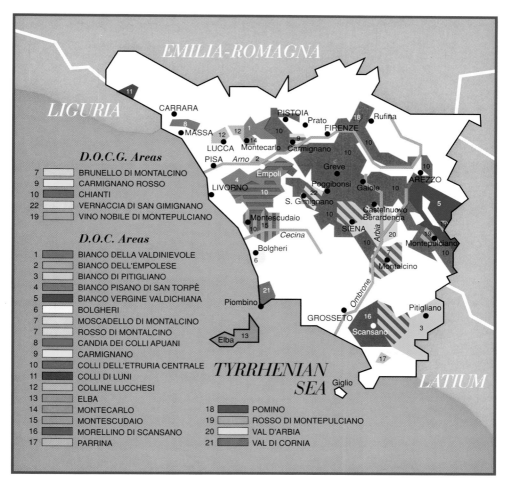

D.O.C.G. Areas

7	BRUNELLO DI MONTALCINO
9	CARMIGNANO ROSSO
10	CHIANTI
22	VERNACCIA DI SAN GIMIGNANO
19	VINO NOBILE DI MONTEPULCIANO

D.O.C. Areas

1	BIANCO DELLA VALDINIEVOLE
2	BIANCO DELL'EMPOLESE
3	BIANCO DI PITIGLIANO
4	BIANCO PISANO DI SAN TORPÈ
5	BIANCO VERGINE VALDICHIANA
6	BOLGHERI
7	MOSCADELLO DI MONTALCINO
7	ROSSO DI MONTALCINO
8	CANDIA DEI COLLI APUANI
9	CARMIGNANO
10	COLLI DELL'ETRURIA CENTRALE
11	COLLI DI LUNI
12	COLLINE LUCCHESI
13	ELBA
14	MONTECARLO
15	MONTESCUDAIO
16	MORELLINO DI SCANSANO
17	PARRINA
18	POMINO
19	ROSSO DI MONTEPULCIANO
20	VAL D'ARBIA
21	VAL DI CORNIA

What Chianti has in common with all the classified red wines of Tuscany is its major grape variety Sangiovese. In the past varieties were often blended, but today the emphasis is strongly on Sangiovese. When the habitat is right, its superior clones — Montalcino's Brunello, Chianti's Sangioveto and Montepulciano's Prugnolo Gentile — must be ranked with Italy's, and the world's, noblest vines.

Tuscany's wine of greatest stature is Brunello di Montalcino, a DOCG from a fortress town south of Siena with reds of legendary power and longevity that have commanded lofty prices. Conceived by the Biondi Santi family a century ago, Brunello is now produced under scores of labels, representing small farms, established estates and even international corporations. Brunello production averages less than 2 million bottles a year, but

producers also make the DOCs of Rosso di Montalcino (a younger wine from Brunello vines) and sweet white Moscadello di Montalcino (from Moscato).

Not far from Montalcino is Montepulciano with its Vino Nobile. The nobile entered the name centuries ago, apparently in homage to its status among the nobility. The poet Francesco Redi described Montepulciano's red as "king of all wines". After a lapse of decades, Vino Nobile has made an impressive comeback under DOCG and is once again living up to its name. Similar to Chianti in composition, Vino Nobile can stand with the finest reserves. The DOC Rosso di Montepulciano is a younger alternative.

Carmignano rates special mention as a wine singled out for protection by the Grand Duke of Tuscany in 1716. Today this rare red from Sangiovese and Cabernet has qualified as DOCG, though the town's rosé and Vin Santo remain as DOC. Pomino, which was also cited in the decree of 1716, is a high altitude DOC zone with a Chianti-type red and a special white which includes Chardonnay and Pinot. Among numerous other DOC reds, Morellino di Scansano, grown in the coastal hills of the Maremma, seems to have a promising future.

From good vintages, pure Sangiovese wines are rich in body and intricate in flavor with deep ruby-garnet colors. Some are smooth and round almost from the start, but others need years to develop the nuances of bouquet and flavor unique to well-aged Tuscan reds. When conditions aren't right, reds from Sangiovese can be lean, harsh and bitter. That explains why some producers have planted other varieties to complement the natives. Cabernet Sauvignon and Merlot have made progress here

By no means all the fine wines of Tuscany are classified. The production of up-scale vini da tavola, which began as a trend in the 1970s, is now an established fact. Sassicaia and Tignanello were the prototypes, but now there are dozens more that rank among the most esteemed and expensive red wines of Italy.

Tuscan whites rarely enjoyed much prestige in the past, probably because most of them consisted of the pedestrian varieties of Trebbiano and Malvasia. Exceptions to the rule stand out from the crowd. Vernaccia di San Gimignano, from the ancient Vernaccia vine, has enjoyed a rapid revival. The rich Vin Santo, pressed from semidried grapes and aged in small wooden barrels, can be an exquisite — or, sometimes, exotic — dessert or aperitif wine.

The best known white is Galestro, made by a group of producers equipped to process Trebbiano with other varieties in a fresh and fruity table wine that is deliberately light in weight. Recently, whites of more complexity and character have been devised in Tuscany, due to the introduction of such varieties as Chardonnay, Sauvignon and Pinot Bianco and Grigio, all of which are finding comfortable environments in cooler parts of the region's hills.

Since few of the new style wines are classified, a consortium of producers issues certain types under four categories: Predicato del

Muschio for white based on Chardonnay; Predicato del Selvante for white based on Sauvignon Blanc; Predicato di Biturica for red based on Cabernet; Predicato di Cardisco for red based on Sangiovese.

DOCGs (5)

Brunello di Montalcino*	R-Dr, Ag-4, Rs Ag-5
Carmignano*	R-Dr, Ag-1.5, Rs Ag-3
Chianti*	R-Dr, Rs Ag-3 (7 subdistricts: Classico, Colli Aretini, Colli Fiorentini, Colli Senesi, Colline Pisane, Montalbano, Rufina)
Vernaccia di San Gimignano	W-Dr, Rs Ag-1, also Liquoroso W-Sw-Ft
Vino Nobile	R-Dr, Ag-2, Rs Ag-3

DOCs (21)

Bianco della Valdinievole	W-Dr, also Vin Santo W-Sw, Ag-3
Bianco dell'Empolese	W-Dr, also Vin Santo W-Dr/Sw, Ag-3
Bianco di Pitigliano	W-Dr, also Sp
Bianco Pisano di San Torpè	W-Dr, also Vin Santo W-Sw, Ag-3
Bianco Vergine Valdichiana	W-Dr, also Fz/Sp
Bolgheri	P-W-Dr
Candia dei Colli Apuani	W-Dr
Carmignano*	Rosato P-Dr, also Fz; Vin Santo W-Dr/Sw, Ag-3
Colli dell'Etruria Centrale*	R-P-Dr, also Fz (red may be called Vermiglio); Vin Santo W-Dr/Sw, Ag-3
Colli di Luni**	3 types: Bianco W-Dr; Rosso R-Dr, Rs Ag-2; Vermentino W-Dr
Colline Lucchesi	R-W-Dr
Elba	R-W-Dr, also (W) Sp
Montecarlo	R-W-Dr
Montescudaio	R-W-Dr, also Vin Santo W-Sw/Dr, Ag-3
Morellino di Scansano	R-Dr, Rs Ag-2
Moscadello di Montalcino*	W-Sw, also Fz, Ft
Parrina	R-P-W-Dr, Rs (R) Ag-3
Pomino	R-Dr, Ag-1, Rs Ag-3; W-Dr; Vin Santo W-Dr/Sw, Ag-3
Rosso di Montalcino*	R-Dr
Rosso di Montepulciano*	R-Dr
Val d'Arbia	W-Dr, also Vin Santo W-Dr/Sw, Ag-3
Val di Cornia	R-P-W-Dr, Rs (R) Ag-3

* Brunello di Montalcino DOCG covers the same zone as Moscadello and Rosso di Montalcino DOC; Carmignano DOCG covers the same zone as Carmignano DOC; Chianti DOCG covers the same zone as Colli dell'Etruria Centrale DOC; Vino Nobile di Montepulciano DOCG covers the same zone as Rosso di Montepulciano.
** Note: the Colli di Luni DOC zone centered in Liguria also extends into Tuscany

Red-Dry

Acciaiolo
Alte d'Altesi
Altero
Balifico
Barco Reale
Boscarelli
Bruno di Rocca
Brusco dei Barbi
Ca' del Pazzo
Cabreo Il Borgo
Campaccio
Campora
Castello Banfi
Castelrapiti
Cepparello
Cetinaia
Codirosso
Coltassala
Concerto
Elegia
Flaccianello della Pieve
Fontalloro
For Duke
Gherardino
Ghiaie della Furba
Granchiaia
Grattamacco Rosso
Grifi
Grosso Sanese
Il Sodaccio
Intistieti
I Sodi di San Niccolò
La Corte
La Gioia di Riecine
La Querce
Le Pergole Torte
Le Vignacce
Logaiolo

Messer Pietro di Teuzzi
Mormoreto
Nemo
Nero del Tondo
Ornellaia
Palazzo Altesi
Percarlo
Poggio Brandi
Predicato di Biturica
Predicato di Cardisco
Querciagrande
Ripa delle More
Roncaia
Rosso di Cercatoia
Sammarco
Sangioveto di Coltibuono
Sarmento
Sassicaia
Selezione di Bongoverno
Ser Gioveto
Sòdole
Solaia
Solatio Basilica
Spargolo
Stielle
Tavernelle
Terricci
Tignanello
Tinscvil
Vallocaia
Veneroso
Vigna Il Chiuso
Vigna L'Apparita
Vigna Peperino
Vigorello
Vinattieri Rosso
Vino novello

White-Dry

Ansonica del Giglio
Belcaro
Campo del Sasso
Canonico
Castelrapiti
Fontanelle
Fumaio
Galestro
Grattamacco Bianco
Il Marzocco
Il Vignola
U Sistri
Le Fagge
Le Grance
Libaio
Molino delle Balze
Nebbiano
Poggio alle Gazze
Poggio Garbato
Predicato del Muschio
Predicato del Selvante
Salterio
San Angelo
Solstizio
Terre di Tufo
Torniello
Torricella
Vigna al Poggio
Villa Antinori Bianco
Vinbrusco

Others

Aleatico, *R-Sw*
Falchini Brut, *W-Sp*
Montellori Brut, *W-Sp*
Sarpinello, *W-Sp*
Sassolato, *W-Sw*
Villa di Capezzana Brut, *W-Sp*

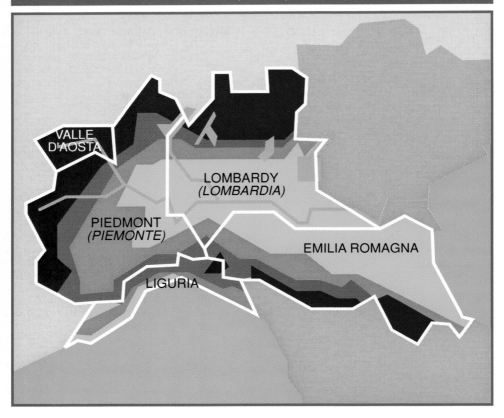

*T*he five regions of north-central and northwest Italy cover much of the great arc of the Alps and Apennines that walls in the Po as it flows east through its broad valley to the Adriatic. The types of wine — like the topography, soil and climate — vary to extremes in these regions, which are grouped rather loosely as neighbors but, in true Italian style, maintain their own proud identities.

This most affluent part of Italy comprises the "industrial triangle" between Milan, Turin and the Mediterranean port of Genoa and the agriculturally fluent flatlands of the Po and its tributaries. Since property is valuable and mountains take up a major share of space, vineyards are confined and wine is a commodity that must be either financially or spiritually rewarding. Yet between the cool terraces of the Alps and the often torrid fields of the Po basin, contrasts abound. Along with some of Italy's most revered bottles can be found some of its most frivolous. But whether the label says Barolo or Lambrusco, the producer probably takes his work seriously.

Between them, the five regions produce about 20% of Italy's total wine and account for about 30% of the DOC. Emilia-Romagna contributes heavily with the fourth largest output among regions after Apulia, Sicily and the Veneto. Piedmont stands tall in the quality field with the most DOC or DOCG zones of any region, as well as the most classified vineyards, even though it ranks only seventh in overall production.

Piedmont dwarfs its neighbors of Valle d'Aosta and Liguria which, by Italian standards at least, are mere dabblers in wine. Valle d'Aosta, the smallest region, produces by far the lowest volume of wine from its rocky slopes. Its DOC output is surpassed by some single wineries in other regions. Liguria, with little space for vines between the mountains and the Mediterranean, is second from the last in production, offering wines that are rarely more than esoteric.

Despite the proximity of France, whose vines have been warmly welcomed elsewhere in Italy, growers in Piedmont, Valle d'Aosta and Liguria prefer their own vines and tend to make wine in their own style. Piedmont's host of worthy natives includes Barbera, Dolcetto, Grignolino, Freisa, Cortese, Arneis, Brachetto, the Canelli clone of Moscato (for Asti Spumante) and the noblest of them all in Nebbiolo (source of Barolo, Barbaresco and Gattinara).

The vines of Valle d'Aosta often have French names — Petit Rouge, Gros Vien, Blanc de Valdigne, for instance — due to the Savoyard history of the region. Liguria favors the local Rossese, Pigato and Vermentino, while working with its own version of Dolcetto, known as Ormeasco.

Lombardy, the most populous region, ranks only twelfth in wine production, but it does boast the largest spread of Pinot vines in the southern Oltrepò Pavese and a major concentration of Nebbiolo vines for the DOC reds of the mountainous Valtellina.

Emilia-Romagna is a prolific region that had been a leading exporter with shipments to America of sweet and bubbly Lambrusco, whose vines spill over the fertile plains of Emilia. But lately growers have been concentrating on distinctive wines from the hills. Best known are the Albana and Sangiovese of Romagna, but gaining notice are Barbera, Cabernet, Chardonnay and Sauvignon from the Apennine foothills of Emilia.

Emilia-Romagna

Regional capital: Bologna.

Provinces: Bologna, Ferrara, Forlì, Modena, Parma, Piacenza, Ravenna, Reggio Emilia.

Emilia-Romagna ranks 6th among the regions in size (22,124 square kilometers) and 8th in population (3,940,000).

Vineyards cover 76,000 hectares (5th) of which registered DOC plots total 26,700 hectares (4th).

Annual wine production of 7,600,000 hectoliters (4th) includes 9% or 700,000 hectoliters DOC or DOCG (5th), of which nearly 75% is red.

*E*milia-Romagna's wines might be considered northern Italy's odd lots, different on the whole from their neighbors', often facile in style, but nearly always refreshingly individualistic. As the hyphenated name reveals, the region consist of two distinct sectors which coincide more or less at the capital of Bologna.

To the west lies Emilia with its prosperous small cities strung like jewels along the ancient Emilian Way — Modena, Reggio, Parma, Fidenza, Fiorenzuola, as far as Picenza. The premier wine here is Lambrusco, in frothy shades of purple to pink, made from grapes grown on high trellised vines mainly in the flatlands south of the Po. Lambrusco is produced at the rate of about 50 million bottles a year in the four DOC zones around Modena and Reggio, though few consumers abroad have tasted these wines in their authentic style. Most Lambrusco shipped away is *amabile* or sweet and sold without an appellation, while most of what is drunk at home is dutifully dry and more often than not DOC. Though there are historical precedents for both types, the dry is considered the unparalleled match for the rich regional cooking.

Even in Emilia's hills, along the Apennine range to the south, the wines are often *frizzante*, made from Malvasia, Trebbiano and Ortrugo into easy, fun-loving whites, or from Barbera and Bonarda into zesty reds of more flavor intensity than Lambrusco. But there is a definite trend in the DOC zones of Colli Piacentini, Colli Bolognesi and Colli di Parma to make still and somewhat serious wines from such varieties as Sauvignon, Chardonnay, the Pinots, Barbera, Cabernet and Merlot. Natural conditions favor wines of depth and finesse but markets seem to favor the lightweights.

East of Bologna lies Romagna, decidedly diverse from Emilia but equally prolific. The plains of the Po basin between Ferrara and Ravenna are noted for fruit, vegetables and ultra high-yield vines, most of which are sources of blending wines. The hills south of Imola, Faenza, Forlì, Cesena and Rimini are known for DOC

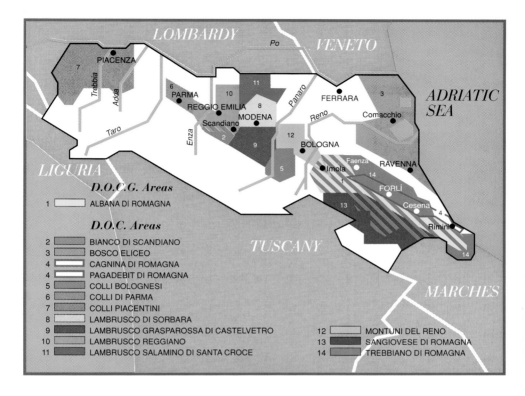

wines, primarily from the native Albana, Sangiovese and Trebbiano.

Albana di Romagna, which emerged in 1987 as Italy's first DOCG white wine, is now most often dry and still with a distinctive almondy undertone and, occasionally, some complexity. Albana's best expression seems to be as a richly sweet passito from partly dried grapes. The traditional semisweet and bubbly versions are usually drunk up near home. Trebbiano (Romagna's is distinct from other vines of the name) is almost always light and fresh, whether still or bubbly, with a fragility that makes it best in its youth.

The local favorite is Sangiovese, usually a medium-bodied red with a certain charm in its straightforward fruity flavor that ends in a bitter bite. Now and then, from certain plots in its *superiore* zone, it becomes a wine of size and depth with the capacity to age gracefully as *riserva*.

In Romagna, too, there are trends toward Sauvignon, Chardonnay, the Pinots and Cabernet. But leading producers devote efforts to developing superior strains of Sangiovese and Albana, while building interest in such rare local wines as the DOC white Pagadebit and red Cagnina and Bosco Eliceo Fortana.

Albana di Romagna	W-Dr/Sw, also Sp as Albana di Romagna DOC

Bianco di Scandiano	W-Dr/Sw-Fz/Sp
Bosco Eliceo	4 types: Bianco W-Dr, also Sw, Fz; Fortana R-Dr, also Sw, Fz; Merlot R-Dr; Sauvignon W-Dr, also Sw, Fz
Cagnina di Romagna	R-Sw
Colli Bolognesi	8 types: Barbera R-Dr, Rs Ag-3; Bianco W-Dr, also Sw, Fz; Cabernet Sauvignon R-Dr, Rs Ag-3; Merlot R-Dr; Pignoletto W-Dr, also Sw, Fz; Pinot Bianco W-Dr, also Sw, Fz; Riesling Italico W-Dr, also Sw, Fz; Sauvignon W-Dr
Colli di Parma	3 types: Malvasia W-Dr-Fz, also Sw, Sp; Rosso R-Dr; Merlot R-Dr, also Fz; Sauvignon W-Dr, also Fz
Colli Piacentini	11 types: Barbera R-Dr, also Fz; Bonarda R-Dr/Sw-Fz; Gutturnio R-Dr, also Sw, Fz; Malvasia W-Dr/Sw-Fz, also Sp; Monterosso Val d'Arda, W-Dr-Fz, also Sw, Sp; Ortrugo W-Dr/Sw-Fz, also Sp; Pinot Grigio W-Dr, also Sp; Pinot Nero R-Dr, also P-W-Sp; Sauvignon W-Dr, also Fz; Trebbianino Val Trebbia W-Dr-Fz, also Sw, Sp; Val Nure W-Dr-Fz, also Sw, Sp
Lambrusco di Sorbara	R-P-Dr-Fz, also Sw
Lambrusco Grasparossa di Castelvetro	R-P-Dr-Fz, also Sw
Lambrusco Reggiano	R-P-Dr-Fz, also Sw
Lambrusco Salamino di Santa Croce	R-P-Dr-Fz, also Sw
Montuni del Reno	W-Dr/Sw-Fz
Pagadebit di Romagna	W-Dr, also Sw, Fz (wine from Bertinoro may be cited)
Sangiovese di Romagna	R-Dr, also Novello, Sup, Rs Ag-2
Trebbiano di Romagna	W-Dr, also Sw, Fz, Sp

Red-Dry		
Alfeo	Ronco dei Ciliegi	Pinot Bianco
Cabernet Sauvignon	Ronco delle Ginestre	Pinot Grigio
Calbanesco	Rosso della Trafila	Ronco del Re
Domus Caia	Stoppa	Sauvignon
Liano		Vicchio
Macchiona	**White-Dry**	
Marzeno di Marzeno	Alionza	**Others**
Picòl Ross	Bianco della Pusterla	Labrusca, P-Sp
Pietramora	Chardonnay	Lambrusco Bianco, W-Sp
Pinot Nero	Jacopo	Picolit, W-Sw
Ronco Casone	Malise	Tarsallo Brut, W-Sp
	Müller Thurgau	Villa Montericco, W-Sw

Liguria

Regional capital: Genoa (Genova).

Provinces: Genova, Imperia, La Spezia, Savona.

Liguria ranks 18th among the regions in size (5,416 square kilometers) and 11th in population (1,770,000).

Vineyards cover 6,000 hectares (19th) of which registered DOC plots total 504 hectares (18th).

Annual wine production of 280,000 hectoliters (19th) includes 5% or 13,000 hectoliters DOC (17th), of which about 75% is white.

*T*he rugged terrain of this slender seaside region makes grape growing a challenge, meaning that vineyards are scattered and limited. Still some of the wines, even if hard to get to, are well worth the search.

The legend among them is Cinqueterre, a white wine made around the "five lands" — fishing villages nestled in the cliffs along the coast north of La Spezia. Vines there have been planted since antiquity on scarcely accessible terraces close enough to the Ligurian Sea to catch the spray from breaking waves. Most Cinqueterre is dry, though the sweet and rare Sciacchetrà is often preferred by those in the know.

Near La Spezia, and the border of Tuscany, is the recent DOC zone of Colli di Luni where red and white wines, notably Vermentino, show promise. Few other wines of the Riviera

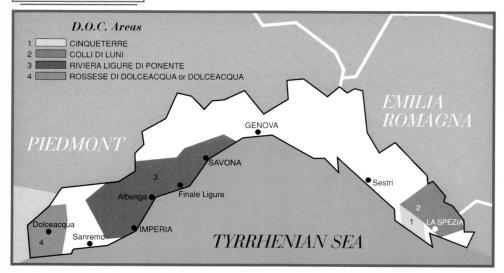

D.O.C. Areas

1 CINQUETERRE
2 COLLI DI LUNI
3 RIVIERA LIGURE DI PONENTE
4 ROSSESE DI DOLCEACQUA or DOLCEACQUA

EMILIA ROMAGNA

PIEDMONT

GENOVA

SAVONA

Sestri

3

Albenga   Finale Ligure

Dolceacqua

Sanremo   IMPERIA

2

1   LA SPEZIA

4

TYRRHENIAN SEA

Levante, the coast to the southeast of Genoa, are known beyond their localities.

Most of Liguria's limited commercial wine production is concentrated along the Ponente coast to the southwest. Until recently, Rossese di Dolceacqua, whose soft fruit and full flavor make it one of most attractive of northern Italian reds, was the only classfied wine. But now the Riviera Ligure di Ponente DOC zone covers the other classic wines of area, the white Pigato and Vermentino and the red Ormeasco (a local Dolcetto) and Rossese di Albenga. Pigato is a white of undeniable class whose prospects seem limited only by lack of vineyard space. Within the large DOC zone are areas with special subdenominations for certain wines: Albenga and Finale for Pigato, Rossese and Vermentino and Riviera dei Fiori for all types.

Most other wines of Liguria are curiosities, local whites and reds that are usually at their best young and close to home. Such rarities as Buzzeto and Granaccia, Coronata and Lumassina are uniquely and proudly Ligurian.

DOCs (4)

Cinqueterre	*W-Dr*, also Sciacchetrà *W-Sw*, also *Ft*, Ag-1
Colli di Luni	3 types: Bianco *W-Dr*; Rosso *R-Dr*, Rs Ag-2; Vermentino *W-Dr*
Riviera Ligure di Ponente	4 types: Ormeasco *R-Dr*, also Sup, Ag-1, Siac-trà *P-Dr*; Pigato *W-Dr*; Rossese *R-Dr*; Vermentino *W-Dr*
Rossese di Dolceacqua or Dolceacqua	*R-Dr*, Sup, Ag-1

OTHER WINES OF NOTE

Red-Dry	*White-Dry*
Barbera	Albachiara
Granaccia di Quiliano	Buzzeto di Quiliano
Terizzo	Coronata
	Lumassina
	Vermentino di Verici
	Vignamare

Lombardy *(LOMBARDIA)*

Regional capital: Milan (Milano).

Provinces: Bergamo, Brescia, Como, Cremona, Mantova, Milano, Pavia, Sondrio, Varese.

Lombardy ranks 4th among the regions in size (23,856 square kilometers) and 1st in population (8,882,000).

Vineyards cover 30,000 hectares (12th) of which registered DOC plots total 16,700 hectares (8th).

Annual wine production of 1,700,000 hectoliters (12th) includes 26% or 450,000 hectoliters DOC (7th), of which there is slightly more red than white.

*A*mong Lombardy's numerous industries wine does not rank high on the list. The citizens of this most populous and well-to-do region seem increasingly disposed toward industrialized versions of agriculture rather than to the more taxing and less profitable hand crafting of fine wines. Also, in a territory that is about half fertile plains and more than a third mountains and lakes, those gentle hills of the sort suited to vines do not abound.

Still, the alpine climate tempered by the lakes of Garda, Iseo, Como and Maggiore in the north and the Apennines which influence the weather to the south have created some highly favorable spots for vines. And, even though output is much less than that of neighboring Veneto, Emilia-Romagna and Piedmont, Lombardy does make some fine wine, a too often neglected share of which is truly excellent.

Just why Lombardians — the eclectic Milanese, in particular — downplay them is hard to explain, but regional bottlings are almost invariably upstaged by the reds of Tuscany and Piedmont and the whites of the Tre Venezie. Most of the 6 million bottles of Nebbiolo reds produced annually in the alpine Valtellina are spirited away by the neighboring Swiss before Italians have a chance at them. The main exception seems to be the *metodo classico* sparkling wines of Franciacorta in the lake district, a zone whose *spumante* is decidedly in vogue.

Lombardy's most productive zone, the Oltrepò Pavese, also ranks as the most abused. Much of its still red and white wines are taken away in bulk or anonymous bottles to restaurants in Milan, Genoa and other cities. Although the Oltrepò is Italy's leading source of Pinot Nero, growers let much of it slip away to Piedmontese and other manufacturers of *brut spumante*, who issue the wines with little regard for origins. Only about 15 percent of the more than 100 million liters produced annually in the Oltrepò is sold as DOC — and then often at bargain prices. Unjustifiably, for some very good wines are made there, not only Pinots, but robust Barbera, Bonarda and Oltrepò Pavese Rosso,

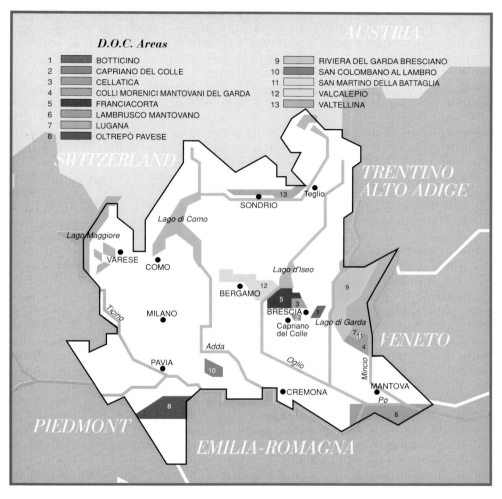

D.O.C. Areas

1	BOTTICINO	9	RIVIERA DEL GARDA BRESCIANO
2	CAPRIANO DEL COLLE	10	SAN COLOMBANO AL LAMBRO
3	CELLATICA	11	SAN MARTINO DELLA BATTAGLIA
4	COLLI MORENICI MANTOVANI DEL GARDA	12	VALCALEPIO
5	FRANCIACORTA	13	VALTELLINA
6	LAMBRUSCO MANTOVANO		
7	LUGANA		
8	OLTREPÒ PAVESE		

plus fruity white Rieslings and Moscatos. A revival in local spumante has been heralded with the trademark of Classese for metodo classico of notable quality.

The Valtellina earns more respect abroad. Bottles of the four *superiore* appellations — Grumello, Inferno, Sassella and Valgella, each of which represents a small subdistrict — can be found in the United States and United Kingdom, along with a bit of the rich and mellow Sfursat or Sforzato. The Valtellina reds are among the most austere of Nebbiolos, due to the coolness of the terraced mountain vineyards, so steep in places that grapes are hauled in with baskets on cables. But the apparent lightness is deceptive, for some have the strength and stamina to improve for well over a decade.

Good wines are made in the provinces of Bergamo, Mantova and even Milano, but the prize for quality and variety goes to Brescia, which boasts 7 of the region's 13 DOCs: Botticino, Capriano del Colle, Cellatica, Franciacorta, Lugana, Riviera del Garda Bresciano and San Martino della Battaglia. From the shores of Lake Garda come Lugana (which can compare with fine Soave Classico) and the distinctive *rosso* and *chiaretto* of Riviera del Garda that can match the best of Valpolicella and Bardolino. The sturdy reds of Botticino and Cellatica and the smooth Tocai of San Martino have admirers as well.

But by all odds the most admired Lombardian wines of the moment are the *spumanti* of Franciacorta. The zone has a good red from Cabernet, Barbera and Nebbiolo and a good still white from Pinot Bianco and Chardonnay. But the reputation has been built on the outstanding bottle-fermented sparkling wines fashioned by small estates. Also in the area is Italy's largest producer of *metodo classico* Guido Berlucchi, though the *cuvées* for nearly 5 million bottles a year include wines from Trentino-Alto Adige, Oltrepò and Piedmont along with the local. In all, Franciacorta produces about a third of Italy's classical spumante, though most of that is not DOC.

Botticino	*R-Dr*
Capriano del Colle	2 types: Rosso *R-Dr*; Trebbiano *W-Dr*
Cellatica	*R-Dr*
Colli Morenici Mantovani del Garda	3 types: Bianco *W-Dr*; Chiaretto or Rosato *P-Dr*; Rosso or Rubino *R-Dr*
Franciacorta	3 types: Bianco or Pinot *W-Dr*; Rosso *R-Dr*; Spumante *W-Dr-Sp*, also Spumante Rosato or Rosé *P-Dr-Sp*
Lambrusco Mantovano	*R/P-Dr-Fz*, also *Sw*
Lugana	*W-Dr*, also *Sp*
Oltrepò Pavese	14 types: Barbera *R-Dr*, also *Fz*; Bonarda *R-Dr*, also *Sw*, *Fz*; Buttafuoco *R-Dr*, also *Fz*; Cortese *W-Dr*, also *Fz*, *Sp*; Moscato *W-Sw-Fz/Sp*; Moscato Liquoroso *W-Sw-Ft*, also *Dr*; Pinot Grigio *W-Dr*, also *Fz*; Pinot Nero *R-Dr*; Pinot Nero Spumante *W-P-Dr-Sp*; Riesling Italico *W-Dr*, also *Fz*, *Sp*; Riesling Renano *W-Dr*, also *Fz*, *Sp*; Rosato *P-Dr*, also *Fz*; Rosso *R-Dr*, also *Fz*, Rs Ag-2; Sangue di Giuda *R-Dr-Fz*, also *Sw*
Riviera del Garda Bresciano	5 types: Bianco *W-Dr*; Chiaretto *P-Dr*; Groppello *R-Dr*; Rosso *R-Dr*, Sup Ag-1; Spumante Rosato *P-Dr-Sp*
San Colombano al Lambro	*R-Dr*
San Martino della Battaglia	*W-Dr*, also Liquoroso *W-Sw-Dr-Ft*
Valcalepio	*R-Dr*, Ag-2; *W-Dr*
Valtellina	*R-Dr*, Ag-1, also Sfurzat or Sforzato *R-Dr*; Valtellina Superiore (Grumello, Inferno, Sassella, Valgella) *R-Dr*, Ag-2, Rs Ag-4

OTHER WINES OF NOTE

Red-Dry

Barbacarlo, Fz
Bohemi
Cabernet Sauvignon
Casotte
Il Felicino
Le Sincette
Lodovico
Marzemino
Maurizio Zanella
Merlot
Montevecchia Rosso
Noir
Pinèro
Pinot Nero
Ronco di Mompiano
Rosso dei Frati Priori
San Gioan
Solesine
Tajardino

White-Dry

Aurito
Chardonnay
Le Zalte
Montevecchia Bianco
Pinot Bianco
Pinot Grigio
Roccascissa
Uccellanda
Verdea della Tonsa

Others

Berlucchi Cuvée Imperiale, W-Dr-Sp
Carlozadra Brut, W-Dr-Sp
Moscato di Scanzo, R-Sw
Villa Mazzucchelli Brut, W-Dr-Sp

Piedmont (PIEMONTE)

Regional capital: Turin (Torino).

Provinces: Alessandria, Asti, Cuneo, Novara, Torino, Vercelli.

Piedmont ranks 2nd among the regions in size (25,399 square kilometers) and 5th in population (4,395,000).

Vineyards cover 70,000 hectares (6th) of which registered DOC plots total 35,900 hectares (1st).

Annual wine production of 3,700,000 hectoliters (7th) includes 32% or 1,200,000 hectoliters DOC or DOCG (tied for 2nd with Tuscany), almost equally divided between red and white.

*P*iedmont is esteemed above all for its red wines, the regal Barolo and Barbaresco in the forefront. But the best known of the region's wines is the white, sweet, bubbly and widely adored Asti Spumante.

Practically all of Piedmont's classified wines derive from native vines. Besides the noble Nebbiolo—source of Barolo, Barbaresco and Gattinara, which are all DOCG—Barbera ranks as the most popular vine for reds and Dolcetto is admired for its soft, full-flavored wines. Freisa, Grignolino, Brachetto and a host of other varieties round out the honor roll of red wines

Still, among classified wines, whites are equally prominent. First comes Moscato d'Asti and the sparkling Asti Spumante, promoted to DOCG. With an average annual output surpassing 50 million liters annually, it ranks second in volume to Chianti among Italy's classified wines. An established star among dry whites is Gavi from the native Cortese grape.

Italy's westernmost region with borders on Switzerland and France, Piedmont is hemmed in by Alps and Apennines, which explain why its name means "foot of the mountain." Though it ranks only seventh among the regions in total production, in every other way Piedmont is a giant of wine. It has the most DOC-DOCG zones with 38 (taking in many distinct types of wine) and the most vineyards dedicated to classified production. For craftsmanship, respect for tradition and devotion to native vines in their historical habitat, the Piedmontese have no rivals in Italy.

The region's climate is rigid by Italian standards, with distinct changes of season. Winters are cold with plenty of snow; summers are usually warm and dry; spring and fall are usually cool with fog normal at harvest time. Most vineyards are located in two major areas; the Langhe and Monferrato hills which are connected to the Apennines in the southeast and the foothills of the Alps to the north between Lake Maggiore and Valle d'Aosta.

The focal point of premium production is the town of Alba on the Tanaro River. In the nearby Langhe hills Barolo (king of wines

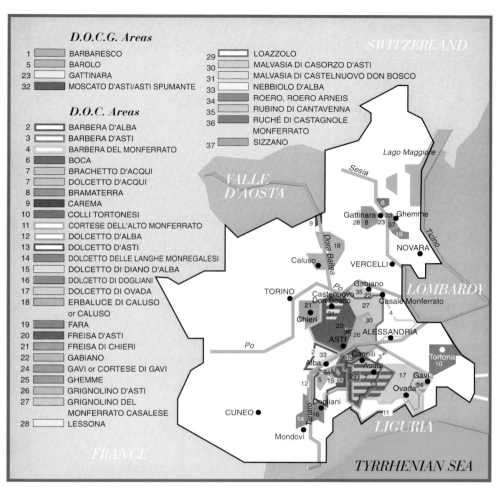

D.O.C.G. Areas

1	BARBARESCO
5	BAROLO
23	GATTINARA
32	MOSCATO D'ASTI/ASTI SPUMANTE

D.O.C. Areas

2	BARBERA D'ALBA
3	BARBERA D'ASTI
4	BARBERA DEL MONFERRATO
6	BOCA
7	BRACHETTO D'ACQUI
7	DOLCETTO D'ACQUI
8	BRAMATERRA
9	CAREMA
10	COLLI TORTONESI
11	CORTESE DELL'ALTO MONFERRATO
12	DOLCETTO D'ALBA
13	DOLCETTO D'ASTI
14	DOLCETTO DELLE LANGHE MONREGALESI
15	DOLCETTO DI DIANO D'ALBA
16	DOLCETTO DI DOGLIANI
17	DOLCETTO DI OVADA
18	ERBALUCE DI CALUSO or CALUSO
19	FARA
20	FREISA D'ASTI
21	FREISA DI CHIERI
22	GABIANO
24	GAVI or CORTESE DI GAVI
25	GHEMME
26	GRIGNOLINO D'ASTI
27	GRIGNOLINO DEL MONFERRATO CASALESE
28	LESSONA
29	LOAZZOLO
30	MALVASIA DI CASORZO D'ASTI
31	MALVASIA DI CASTELNUOVO DON BOSCO
33	NEBBIOLO D'ALBA
34	ROERO, ROERO ARNEIS
35	RUBINO DI CANTAVENNA
36	RUCHÉ DI CASTAGNOLE MONFERRATO
37	SIZZANO

SWITZERLAND

VALLE D'AOSTA

LOMBARDY

LIGURIA

FRANCE

TYRRHENIAN SEA

Lago Maggiore

Sesia

Ticino

Gattinara · 25 Ghemme
28 8 23 37
19
NOVARA
Dora Baltea
18
Caluso
VERCELLI ·
Po
Gabiano
TORINO
Castenuovo 35 22
Don Bosco 27 Casale Monferrato
21 31
Chieri 4
20 30
36 26 ALESSANDRIA
ASTI
Po
2 33 Canelli 3
Alba 32 Acqui Tortona
34 10
12 5 15 32 29 7 17 Gavi
13 Ovada 24
CUNEO · Dogliani 11
14 16
Tanaro
Mondovì

---

and wine of kings) is produced at the rate of about 6 million bottles a year and Barbaresco, which many experts rate its equal, rarely reaches half that. Both come from Nebbiolo, which gives them the powerful structure that makes them capable of improving for many years from fine vintages such as '90, '89, '88, '86, '85, '82, '79, '78, and '71.

The traditional Barolo and Barbaresco were admired almost as cult wines, though often criticized as too elaborate for modern palates. But the combination of a series of fine vintages and newly studied techniques among winemakers, many of them young, seems to be changing the old-fashioned image. Barolo and Barbaresco have retained their ample dimensions while becoming better balanced and more approachable than before. The Alba area is renowned for its smooth, supple Dolcetto under

several appellations, and for first-rate Nebbiolo and white Arneis from the Roero hills, as well as table wines of class sometimes under the name Langhe.

But the most surprising progress in both the Alba and Asti areas has been made with the ubiquitous Barbera, which after years of being considered common has rapidly become chic. Certain aged Barberas from choice plots around Asti and Alba have emerged to stand comparison with fine Nebbiolo reds. Piedmontese drink more red wine than white, and about half of the red is Barbera, which can also be attractive in youthfully fruity and bubbly versions. Three other red wines that have recovered after decades of decline are the pale Grignolino, the often frizzante Freisa and the sweet and bubbly Brachetto from Acqui.

In the other major area of Nebbiolo production, the hills to the north, more modern styles are emerging in such reds as Ghemme, Carema, Lessona, Sizzano, Fara and the long vaunted Gattinara, which has become DOCG.

Piedmont ranks with Italy's leading producers of sparkling wines. Foremost among them is Asti Spumante, the world's most popular sweet sparkling wine. The market for this fragrant white is actually larger abroad than in Italy. In fact, worldwide demand is so great that a shortage of Moscato di Canelli grapes has developed. The region is also a major producer of dry sparkling wines by both the classical and charmat methods, though only rarely do the Pinot and Chardonnay grapes originate in the region. Most come from the neighboring Oltrepó Pavese in Lombardy or from Trentino Alto-Adige.

Among still whites, Gavi has emerged as one of Italy's most coveted, with a crisp, lively style. Admirers consider it one of the best with seafood. Arneis continues to gain ground in Roero, where the light, zesty Favorita is also beginning to emerge. Some predict a revival of the ancient white Erbaluce di Caluso from near Turin.

Although Piedmontese growers were among the first to experiment with such outside varieties as Cabernet and the Pinots early in the19th century, these vines largely faded from favor. Just recently, though, Cabernet Sauvignon, the Pinots and especially Chardonnay have shown unusual promise as table wines. But admirers have noted that, despite their vines' universal status, the wines bear a stamp that is unmistakably Piedmontese.

DOCGs (4)

Barbaresco	*R-Dr*, Ag-2, Rs Ag-4
Barolo	*R-Dr*, Ag-3, Rs Ag-5
Gattinara	*R-Dr*, Ag-3, Rs Ag-4
Moscato d'Asti/ Asti Spumante	*W-Sw-Fz*, Asti Spumante *W-Sw-Sp*

Barbera d'Alba	*R-Dr*, Sup Ag-1
Barbera d'Asti	*R-Dr*, also *Fz*, Sup Ag-1
Barbera del Monferrato	*R-Dr*, also *Fz*, Sup Ag-2
Boca	*R-Dr*, Ag-3
Brachetto d'Acqui	*R-Sw-Fz/Sp*
Bramaterra	*R-Dr*, Ag-2, Rs Ag-3
Carema	*R-Dr*, Ag-4
Colli Tortonesi	2 types: Barbera *R-Dr*, Sup Ag-2; Cortese *W-Sw*, also *Fz*, *Sp*
Cortese dell'Alto Monferrato	*W-Dr*, also *Fz*, *Sp*
Dolcetto d'Acqui	*R-Dr*, Sup Ag-1
Dolcetto d'Alba	*R-Dr*, Sup Ag-1
Dolcetto d'Asti	*R-Dr*, Sup Ag-1
Dolcetto delle Langhe Monregalesi	*R-Dr*, Sup Ag-1
Dolcetto di Diano d'Alba	*R-Dr*, Sup Ag-1
Dolcetto di Dogliani	*R-Dr*, Sup Ag-1
Dolcetto di Ovada	*R-Dr*, Sup Ag-1
Erbaluce di Caluso or Caluso	2 types: Erbaluce *W-Dr*, also *Sp*; Caluso Passito *W-Sw*, also *Ft*, Ag-5
Fara	*R-Dr*, Ag-3
Freisa d'Asti	*R-Dr/Sw-Fz/Sp*, Sup Ag-1
Freisa di Chieri	*R-Dr/Sw-Fz/Sp*
Gabiano	*R-Dr*, Rs Ag-2
Gavi or Cortese di Gavi	*W-Dr*, also *Fz*, *Sp*
Ghemme	*R-Dr*, Ag-4
Grignolino d'Asti	*R-Dr*
Grignolino del Monferrato Casalese	*R-Dr*
Lessona	*R-Dr*, Ag-2
Loazzolo	*W-Sw*, Ag-2
Malvasia di Casorzo d'Asti	*R-Sw-Fz/Sp*
Malvasia di Castelnuovo Don Bosco	*R-Sw-Fz/Sp*
Nebbiolo d'Alba	*R-Dr*, Sup Ag-1, also *Sw-Fz/Sp*
Roero	2 types: Roero *R-Dr*, also Sup; Arneis di Roero *W-Dr*, also *Sp*

Rubino di Cantavenna	R-Dr
Ruchè di Castagnole Monferrato	R-Dr
Sizzano	R-Dr, Ag-3

OTHER WINES OF NOTE

Red-Dry

Airone
Arte
Barengo
Barilot
Bonarda
Bricco del Drago
Bricco della Bigotta
Bricco dell'Uccellone
Bricco Manzoni
Bricco Viole
Canavese Rosso
Crichët Pajé
Croutin
Darmagi
Favot
Fioretto
I Fossaretti
Il Giorgione
La Monella
Le Taragne
Maria Gioana
Martina
Mondaccione

Monprà
Montruc
Möt Ziflon
Opera Prima
Orbello
Passum
Piccone
Policalpo
Rocca di Mattarello
Rubello di Salabue
San Guglielmo
Spanna
Tupium
Vigna Arborina
Vigna dell'Angelo
Vigna Larigi
Vignaserra
Villa Pattono
Vino novello

White-Dry

Alteni di Brassica
Bric Buschet
Canavese Bianco

Favorita
Gaia & Rey
Giarone
Greco
L'Angelica
Mimosa
Monteriolo
Morino
Piodilei
Plissé
Rossj-Bass
Timorasso

Others

Casarito, W-Sw
Casortino, R-Sw
Moscato di Strevi, W-Sw
Pelaverga, P-Dr
Pian dei Sogni, R-Sw
Solativa, W-Sw
Spumante Brut, W-Dr-Sp, also P
Vigneto Cariola, W-Sw

Note: Many *vini da tavola* carrying the name of a grape variety or color or type should be included under the proposed DOCs on Langhe, Monferrato and Piemonte.

Regional capital and single province: Aosta.

Valle d'Aosta is the smallest of Italy's 20 regions in size (3,262 square kilometers) and population (113,000).

Vineyards cover 925 hectares (20th) of which registered DOC plots total 66 hectares (20th).

Annual wine production of 39,000 hectoliters (20th) includes 3.5% or 2,400 hectoliters DOC (19th), of which about two-thirds is red.

*T*his tiniest of regions, tucked into Italy's mountainous northwest corner against the borders of Switzerland and France, has precious little space for vines on its stony alpine terraces. But the minuscule amounts of wine it does produce are distinct from anything else in Italy or its foreign neighbors.

A regionwide DOC known as Valle d'Aosta or Vallée d'Aoste covers 21 types of wine whose names are given in Italian and French, the official second language. These include the long-standing DOCs of Donnaz and Enfer d'Arvier, as well as the white wines of Morgex and La Salle, whose vineyards in the shadow of Mont Blanc are reputed to be the highest in Europe.

But whether Valle d'Aosta's wines are classified or not, they could never be more than curios that are most compelling when drunk on the spot. Grape varieties range from Piedmontese (Nebbiolo, Dolcetto, Moscato) to French (the Pinots, Gamay), to the teutonic Müller Thurgau called in for alpine duty. But the

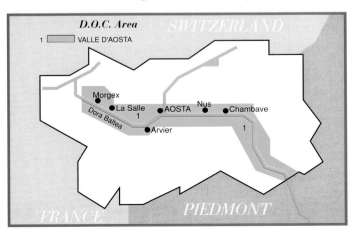

most intriguing wines of Valle d'Aosta stem from varieties it calls its own. These include the Petit Rouge of Enfer d'Arvier and Torrette, the Blanc de Valdigne of Morgex and la Salle, the Petite Arvine of the white Vin du Conseil, the Vien for the red wine of Nus and the Malvoisie (apparently a mutation of Pinot Gris) for rare dessert white of Nus.

DOC (1)

Valle d'Aosta or Vallée d'Aoste	21 types: Arnad Montjovet *R-Dr*, Sup Ag-1; Bianco or Blanc *W-Dr*, also *Fz*; Blanc de Morgex et de La Salle *W-Dr*, also *Sp*; Chambave Moscato or Muscat *W-Dr*, also Passito or Flétri *W-Sw*, Ag-1; Chambave Rosso or Rouge *R-Dr*; Chardonnay *W-Dr*; Donnaz or Donnas *R-Dr*, Ag-2; Enfer d'Arvier *R-Dr*; Fumin *R-Dr*; Gamay *R-Dr*; Müller Thurgau *W-Dr*; Novello *R-Dr*; Nus Malvoisie *W-Dr*, also Passito or Flétri *W-Sw*, Ag-1; Nus Rosso or Rouge *R-Dr*; Petite Arvine *W-Dr*; Petit Rouge *R-Dr*; Pinot Grigio or Pinot Gris *W-Dr*; Pinot Nero or Pinot Noir *R-Dr*, also *W-Dr*; Premetta *R-Dr*; Rosso or Rosato *R-Dr* or *P-Dr*; Torrette *R-Dr*, also *Sup*
Note: names and labels may be in Italian or French	

OTHER WINES OF NOTE

Red-Dry	White-Dry	Others
Barnet	Blanc de Cossan	Malvoisie de Cossan, *W-Sw*
Grenache	Blanc Ollignan	Passito Le Muraglie, *W-Sw*
La Sabla	La Gazzella	
Merlot	Riesling	
Rosso Le Muraglie	Vin du Conseil	
Sang des Salasses		
Syrah		

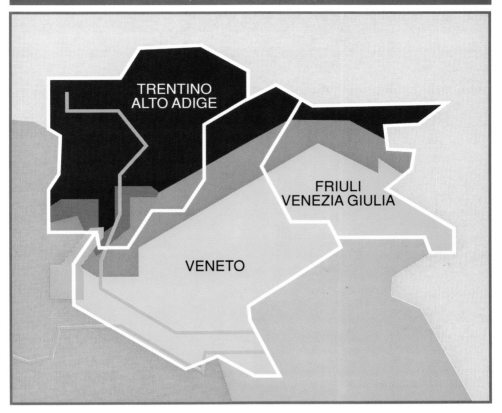

*T*he three northeastern regions, known collectively as the Tre Venezie or simply the Venezie, set the pace in Italy in the crafting of modern wines. Together they produce more classified wine than any other section of the country — more than a third of the DOC, the more remarkable when you consider that they account for less than a sixth of the nation's total production. The Veneto is first in volume of DOC and Trentino-Alto Adige leads in percentage of its total, while Friuli-Venezia Giulia enhances the classified ranks with its stylishly contemporary white wines.

The technology of winemaking overall is more sophisticated and better organized here than elsewhere, thanks in part to the continuing demand from neighboring Germany, Austria and Switzerland, as well as more distant markets such as the United States and United Kingdom. Two of Italy's leading wine schools are here (at San Michele all'Adige in Trentino and Conegliano in Veneto). The world's largest vine nursery is at Rauscedo in Friuli. The nation's most important wine fair, Vinitaly, is held each spring in Verona.

The determinant quality factor in all three regions is the climate influenced by the Alps, of which the Venezie are on the sunny side, protected from the damp cold of northern Europe. Vineyard conditions range from cool at high altitudes to warm in the plains near the Adriatic Sea and along the valley of the Po, Piave and Adige rivers.

Admirers of Soave, Pinot Grigio, Chardonnay, Tocai and other popular whites are often surprised to learn that the Venezie make more red wine than white. But, as elsewhere, the worldwide demand for white wine is rapidly changing that pattern. Friuli and the Veneto have reversed earlier patterns and now make more white wine than red under DOC.

Although the culture of the Venezie, like the name, was determined by the ancient Venetian Republic, strong influences can be felt from Austria and Slovenia. One result is a cosmopolitan mix of vine varieties. Growers here work with an amazing assortment of native and imported vines to produce what are indisputably a majority of Italy's finer white wines, a number of the better rosés and a multitude of reds, ranging from the young and simplistic to the aged and complex.

Verona's Soave, Valpolicella and Bardolino are the best known of the many DOCs. They derive almost entirely from native varieties. But in the central and eastern Veneto and Friuli imported varieties — such as Merlot, Cabernet, the Pinots, Chardonnay and Sauvignon — are vying successfully for vineyard space against the local Tocai, Prosecco, Verduzzo, Refosco and Raboso.

In Trentino-Alto Adige red wines prevail, dominated by the ubiquitous Schiava or Vernatsch, though the more distinguished Teroldego, Lagrein and Marzemino hold their own against Cabernet, Merlot and Pinot Nero. The emerging favorites, however, are the white Chardonnay, Pinots and Sauvignon.

Since so many varietal wines are produced, in all three regions, the practice has been to group the wines under a single DOC name for a geographical area, such as the Veneto's Piave, Friuli's Collio Goriziano, and the provincial appellation of Trentino and Alto Adige. Though the lists may be long, this geographical identity seems to aid consumers in connecting places with grape varieties.

Veneto

Regional capital: Venice (Venezia).

Provinces: Belluno, Padova, Rovigo, Treviso, Venezia, Verona, Vicenza.

The Veneto ranks 8th among the regions in size (18,364 square kilometers) and 6th in population (4,371,000).

Vineyards cover 90,000 hectoliters (3rd) of which registered DOC plots total 35,400 hectares (2nd).

Annual wine production of 8,500,000 hectoliters (3rd) includes 20% or 1,700,000 hectoliters DOC (1st), of which about 55% is white.

Venice's region is Italy's leader in the production and commerce of classified wine. A major share of the DOC (which represents about 225 million bottles a year) consists of the Verona trio of Soave, Bardolino and Valpolicella. But since DOC represents less than a fifth of the region's total, the Veneto also figures as a major producer and exporter of unclassified table wines, often of moderate price.

There are three general areas of premium production: the western province of Verona in the hills between Lake Garda and the town of Soave; the central hills in the provinces of Vicenza, Padova and Treviso; the eastern plains of the Piave and Tagliamento river basins along the Adriatic coast northeast of Venice.

Verona's classic wines are bona fides natives. Soave, from Garganega and Trebbiano di Soave, is usually dry and still, though spumante and sweet Recioto versions are also prescribed. Third after Chianti and Asti Spumante in volume among classified wines (with some 50 million liters a year), Soave has long been Italy's most popular DOC wine abroad.

Valpolicella, made from a blend of Corvina, Rondinella and Molinara, has been fourth in volume among DOCs with about 35 million liters. Valpolicella is noted as a full and fruity red to drink relatively young, though grapes from its vineyards in the hills north of Verona can also be partly dried and made into the richly dry Amarone della Valpolicella or the opulently sweet Recioto della Valpolicella. Amarone, amply structured and long on the palate, ranks with Italy's most authoritative red wines. Bardolino, from the same basic grapes as Valpolicella, is enviably easy to drink, whether in the light red or dark pink *chiaretto* version. Recent popularity is due largely to its emergence as Italy's first classified novello. This DOC on the shores of Lake Garda also ranks high on the list of volume with about 20 million liters a year.

Another Veronese DOC of note is Bianco di Custoza, strikingly similar to Soave. A recent DOC made between Verona and Vicen-

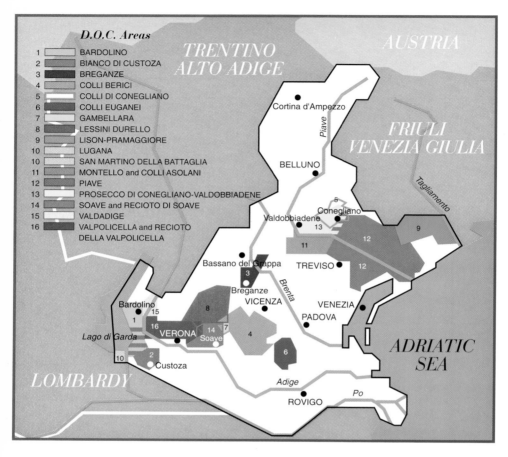

D.O.C. Areas

1	BARDOLINO
2	BIANCO DI CUSTOZA
3	BREGANZE
4	COLLI BERICI
5	COLLI DI CONEGLIANO
6	COLLI EUGANEI
7	GAMBELLARA
8	LESSINI DURELLO
9	LISON-PRAMAGGIORE
10	LUGANA
10	SAN MARTINO DELLA BATTAGLIA
11	MONTELLO and COLLI ASOLANI
12	PIAVE
13	PROSECCO DI CONEGLIANO-VALDOBBIADENE
14	SOAVE and RECIOTO DI SOAVE
15	VALDADIGE
16	VALPOLICELLA and RECIOTO DELLA VALPOLICELLA

za is Lessini Durello, a steely dry white, usually sparkling, that seems destined for wider recognition. A trend in the Verona area is to make alternative wines of distinction. Some innovative reds are gaining prominence, notably the so-called *ripasso* types made from the base of Valpolicella refermented with the pomace of Amarone.

The Veneto's central hills take in several DOC zones. Near Vicenza are Gambellara, with whites similar to those of neighboring Soave, and Colli Berici, where varietal wines from Tocai, the Pinots, Merlot and Cabernet prevail. Also in the province is Breganze, where Cabernet and whites from the Pinots and Chardonnay and the sweet Torcolato stand out. Near Padova are the Colli Euganei, whose sheer slopes render a range of varietals.

Treviso's province takes in the hills northwest of Venice between the towns of Conegliano and Valdobbiadene, noted for the popular Prosecco, a dry to lightly sweet white, usually

bubbly. A refined version is known as Cartizze. The adjacent Montello e Colli Asolani zone is noted for Prosecco, Cabernet and Merlot, as well as the renowned *vino da tavola* Venegazzù della Casa. Producers of Prosecco, already well versed in sparkling wine, have been increasing Pinot and Chardonnay spumanti, usually dry and made either by the tank fermentation or the classical method.

The plains northeast of Venice take in the Piave DOC zone, where Merlot and Cabernet dominate an expanding range of trendy varietals, though the local red Raboso and white Verduzzo still attract admirers. Lison-Pramaggiore (previously noted for white Tocai and Cabernet and Merlot) now also has a full list of varietals.

In red wines, Merlot and Cabernet Franc have been the workhorse varieties of the central and eastern Veneto for decades, often in light and easy wines to drink young. But some producers have been blending the two, increasingly with Cabernet Sauvignon, and aging the wine in small barrels to develop greater style and complexity. Throughout the region the recent emphasis is on white wines. Pinot Grigio, Sauvignon and especially Chardonnay are gaining ground.

DOCs (14)*

Bardolino	R-Dr, also novello, Sup Ag-1; Chiaretto P-Dr, also Sp
Bianco di Custoza	W-Dr, also Sp
Breganze	7 types: Bianco W-Dr; Cabernet R-Dr; Pinot Bianco W-Dr; Pinot Grigio W-Dr; Pinot Nero R-Dr; Rosso R-Dr; Vespaiolo W-Dr
Colli Berici	7 types: Cabernet R-Dr, Rs Ag-3; Garganega W-Dr; Merlot R-Dr; Pinot Bianco W-Dr; Sauvignon W-Dr; Tocai Bianco W-Dr; Tocai Rosso R-Dr
Colli di Conegliano	4 types: Bianco W-Dr; Rosso R-Dr, Ag-2; Marzemino Passito di Refrontolo R-Sw, also Fz; Torchiato di Fregona W-Dr/Sw, Ag-1;
Colli Euganei	7 types: Bianco W-Dr, also Sw, Sp; Cabernet R-Dr, Sup Ag-1; Merlot R-Dr, Sup Ag-1; Moscato W-Sw-Fz/Sp; Pinot Bianco W-Dr; Rosso R-Dr; Tocai Italico W-Dr
Gambellara	3 types: Bianco W-Dr; Recioto di Gambellara W-Sw, also Sp; Vin Santo di Gambellara W-Sw, Ag-2
Lessini Durello	W-Dr, also Sp
Lison-Pramaggiore	12 types: Cabernet R-Dr, also Sp, Rs Ag-3; Cabernet Franc R-Dr, also Sp, Rs Ag-3; Cabernet Sauvignon R-Dr, also Sp, Rs Ag-3;Chardonnay W-Dr, also Sp; Merlot R-Dr, also Sp, Rs Ag-2; Pinot Bianco W-Dr, also Sp; Pinot Grigio W-Dr, also Sp; Refosco dal Peduncolo Rosso R-Dr; Riesling Italico W-Dr, also Sp; Sauvignon W-Dr, also Sp; Tocai Italico W-Dr, also Sp; Verduzzo W-Dr, also Sp
Montello e Colli Asolani	9 types: Cabernet R-Dr, Sup Ag-2; Cabernet Franc R-Dr, Sup Ag-2; Cabernet Sauvignon R-Dr, Sup Ag-2; Chardonnay W-Dr, also Sp; Merlot R-Dr, Sup Ag-2; Pinot Bianco W-Dr, also Sp; Pinot Grigio W-Dr; Prosecco W-Dr/Sw-Fz/Sp; Rosso R-Dr, Sup Ag-2.

Piave or Vini del Piave	10 types: Cabernet *R-Dr*, Rs Ag-3; Cabernet Sauvignon *R-Dr*, Rs Ag-3; Chardonnay *W-Dr*; Merlot *R-Dr*, Rs Ag-2; Pinot Bianco *W-Dr*; Pinot Grigio *W-Dr*; Pinot Nero *R-Dr*; Raboso *R-Dr*, Ag-3; Tocai *W-Dr*; Verduzzo *W-Dr*
Prosecco di Conegliano-Valdobbiadene	*W-Dr/Sw-Fz/Sp*; Superiore di Cartizze *W-Dr/Sw-Fz/Sp*
Soave	*W-Dr*; also *Sp*; Recioto di Soave *W-Sw, also Sp-Ft*
Valpolicella (also Valpolicella-Valpantena)	*R-Dr*, Sup Ag-1; Amarone della Valpolicella *R-Dr, Ag-2*; Recioto della Valpolicella *R-Sw, also Sp, Ft*

* Note: the Lugana and San Martino della Battaglia DOC zones, centered in Lombardy, extend into the Veneto; Valdadige extends into the Veneto from Trentino-Alto Adige.

OTHER WINES OF NOTE

Red-Dry	White-Dry	Others
Alzero	Bianco San Pietro	Amabile del Cerè, *W-Sw*
Borgo di Peuma	Bianco Toara	Acininobili, *W-Sw*
Camoi	Capitel San Rocco Bianco	Campociesa, *W-Sw*
Campofiorin	Catullo	Costa d'Olio, *P-Dr*
Capitel San Rocco Rosso	Chardonnay, also *Sp*	Dindarello, *W-Sw*
Castello Guerrieri	Creso	Fiorgardane, *W-Sw*
Catullo	Dògoli	Spumante Brut, *W/P-Dr-Sp*
Creso	Ferrata	Torcolato, *W-Sw*
Ferrata	Masianco	Vin de la Fabriseria, *W-Sw*
La Poja	Prato di Canzio	
Le Sassine	Verdiso, also *Fz*	
Malbec or Malbeck		
Morago		
Pelara		
Realda		
Refolà		
Venegazzù della Casa		
Vigneto del Falcone		
Villa Giustinian		
Wildbacher		

Friuli-Venezia Giulia

Regional capital: Trieste.

Provinces: Gorizia, Pordenone, Trieste, Udine.

Friuli-Venezia Giulia ranks 17th among the regions in size (7,847 square kilometers) and 15th in population (1,220,000).

Vineyards cover 21,000 hectares (15th) of which registered DOC plots total 12,300 hectares (9th).

Annual wine production of 1,100,000 hectoliters (15th) includes 40% or 430,000 hectoliters DOC (8th), of which more than 60% is white.

*T*he compact region of Friuli-Venezia Giulia, which borders on Austria, Slovenia and Croatia, is the realm of Italy's new-style white wine. Drawing from worthy native varieties and the noblest of the international array, Friulians have applied studied vineyard techniques and avant-garde enology to the production of highly distinctive whites, as well as some eminently attractive reds.

Friuli has two DOC zones of exceptional status in Collio Goriziano, or simply Collio, and Colli Orientali del Friuli, adjacent areas that follow the border of Slovenia from Gorizia northwest to Tarcento. A highly favorable environment is created on the terraced slopes, called *ronchi*, by the exchange of Adriatic and alpine currents. Carso is a unique zone in the hills above the seaport and regional capital of Trieste. The other four DOC zones cover low hills or plains, but quality there can also be convincing.

Nearly all the wines included in the seven DOC categories are varietals. Usually about 40% of Friuli's total production is DOC, but whether or not wines are classified they tend to be reliable. Only the Grave del Friuli zone, which produces nearly 20 million liters a year to stand with the top ten DOCs in volume, is big by national standards.

Friuli has built a glowing reputation in Italy and abroad for white wines. Tocai Friulano has been dominant, a fine variety, which, despite its name, seems to be a native of Friuli with no parental links to other wines known as Tokay or Tokaji. The local Malvasia, Ribolla and Verduzzo can be intriguing, as can such long-established imported varieties as Chardonnay, Sauvignon, the Pinots, Traminer and Riesling.

The Friulian style in whites favors the exquisitely fresh and fruity, with delicate fragrance and flavor that express clear varietal character. Many producers consider their whites to be too pure and linear to benefit from wood aging. The Friulian style has been on target for the national market, which seems to favor the flavors and names of pure varietals. There are exceptions to the rule,

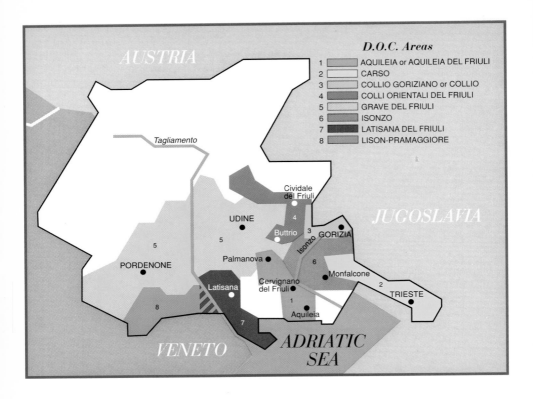

D.O.C. Areas

1	AQUILEIA or AQUILEIA DEL FRIULI
2	CARSO
3	COLLIO GORIZIANO or COLLIO
4	COLLI ORIENTALI DEL FRIULI
5	GRAVE DEL FRIULI
6	ISONZO
7	LATISANA DEL FRIULI
8	LISON-PRAMAGGIORE

though, in certain white table wines which gain depth and complexity from blending, wood aging and other artistic touches.

Friulian reds were traditionally light and fruity, best to drink within two to five years of the harvest. This applies to the predominant Merlot and Cabernet Franc, as well as Pinot Nero and the prominent native variety of Refosco. But certain winemakers have heightened structure and nuance by blending Cabernet, Merlot and other varieties and aging the wine in small, new oak barrels.

Friulians have shown an encouraging tendency to rediscover certain varieties that had been neglected and to revive them. Foremost among the legends is Picolit, a white that ranked as one of Europe's finest sweet wines around 1800 when it was favored by the Hapsburgs. Despite low yields, Picolit has been coming back. So has Verduzzo, which makes exquisitely light dessert wines in the Colli Orientali. Ribolla Gialla, a native of Collio, has benefited from new methods that make it into a dry white of character. Among the reds are Refosco, which can be made either light and fruity or into a durable wine for aging. Though rare and odd, Franconia and Tazzelenghe make distinctive reds, but perhaps the Schioppettino grape has the greatest quality potential.

Sparkling wines represent a growing field, as winemakers bring not only choice Pinot and Chardonnay grapes into their cuvées but also Ribolla for refined spumante by the classical and charmat methods.

DOCs (7)*

Aquileia or Aquileia del Friuli	14 types: Cabernet *R-Dr*; Cabernet Franc *R-Dr*; Cabernet Sauvignon *R-Dr*; Chardonnay, *W-Dr*, also *Sp*; Merlot *R-Dr*; Pinot Bianco *W-Dr*; Pinot Grigio *W-Dr*; Refosco *R-Dr*; Riesling Renano *W-Dr*; Rosato *P-Dr*; Sauvignon *W-Dr*; Tocai Friulano *W-Dr*; Traminer *W-Dr*; Verduzzo Friulano *W-Dr*
Carso	3 types: Carso *R-Dr*; Carso Malvasia *W-Dr*; Terrano del Carso *R-Dr*
Collio Goriziano or Collio	19 types: Bianco *W-Dr*; Cabernet *R-Dr*, Rs Ag-3; Cabernet Franc *R-Dr*, Rs Ag-3; Cabernet Sauvignon *R-Dr*, Rs Ag-3; Chardonnay *W-Dr*; Malvasia Istriana *W-Dr*; Merlot *R-Dr*, Rs Ag-3; Müller Thurgau *W-Dr*; Picolit *W-Sw*; Pinot Bianco *W-Dr*; Pinot Grigio *W-Dr*; Pinot Nero *R-Dr*, Rs Ag-3; Ribolla Gialla *W-Dr*; Riesling Italico *W-Dr*; Riesling Renano *W-Dr*; Rosso *R-Dr*, Rs Ag-3; Sauvignon *W-Dr*; Tocai Friulano *W-Dr*; Traminer Aromatico *W-Dr*
Colli Orientali del Friuli	20 types: Cabernet *R-Dr*, Rs Ag-2; Cabernet Franc *R-Dr*, Rs Ag-2; Cabernet Sauvignon *R-Dr*, Rs Ag-2; Chardonnay *W-Dr*; Malvasia Istriana Merlot *R-Dr*, Rs Ag-2; Picolit *W-Sw*, Rs Ag-2; Pinot Bianco *W-Dr*; Pinot Grigio *W-Dr*; Pinot Nero *R-Dr*, Rs Ag-2; Ramandolo *W-Sw*, also Classico; Refosco *R-Dr*, Rs Ag-2; Ribolla Gialla *W-Dr*; Riesling Renano *W-Dr*; Rosato *P-Dr*; Sauvignon *W-Dr*; Schioppettino *R-Dr*; Tocai Friulano *W-Dr*; Traminer Aromatico *W-Dr*; Verduzzo Friulano *W-Dr/Sw*
Grave del Friuli	15 types: Cabernet *R-Dr*; Cabernet Franc *R-Dr*; Cabernet Sauvignon *R-Dr*; Chardonnay *W-Dr*; Merlot *R-Dr*; Pinot Bianco *W-Dr*; Pinot Grigio *W-Dr*; Pinot Nero, *R-Dr*; Refosco *R-Dr*; Riesling Renano *W-Dr*; Rosato *P-Dr*; Sauvignon *W-Dr*; Tocai Friulano *W-Dr*; Traminer Aromatico *W-Dr*; Verduzzo Friulano *W-Dr/Sw*, also *Fz*
Isonzo	19 types: Bianco *W-Dr*, also *Sw, Fz*; Cabernet *R-Dr*; Cabernet Franc *R-Dr*; Cabernet Sauvignon *R-Dr*; Chardonnay *W-Dr*; Franconia *R-Dr*; Malvasia Istriana *W-Dr*; Merlot *R-Dr*; Pinot Bianco *W-Dr*, also Pinot Spumante *W-Dr-Sp*; Pinot Grigio *W-Dr*; Pinot Nero *R-Dr*; Refosco *R-Dr*; Riesling Italico *W-Dr*; Riesling Renano *W-Dr*; Rosso *R-Dr*, also *Sw, Fz*; Sauvignon *W-Dr*; Tocai Friulano *W-Dr*; Traminer Aromatico *W-Dr*; Verduzzo Friulano *W-Dr*
Latisana del Friuli	13 types: Cabernet *R-Dr*; Cabernet Franc *R-Dr*; Cabernet Sauvignon *R-Dr*; Chardonnay *W-Dr*; Merlot *R-Dr*; Pinot Bianco *W-Dr*; Pinot Grigio *W-Dr*; Refosco *R-Dr*; Rosato *P-Dr*; Sauvignon *W-Dr*; Tocai Friulano *W-Dr*; Traminer Aromatico *W-Dr*; Verduzzo Friulano *W-Dr*

* Note: The Lison-Pramaggiore DOC zone extends from the Veneto into Friuli

Red-Dry	Rujno	Roncuz
	Tazzelenghe or Tacelenghe	St. Jurosa
Agreste	Vigna del Balbo	Soreli
Araldo		Terre Alte
Baredo	**White-Dry**	Vedute di Pradis
Braida Nuova		Vigne delle Letizie
Carantan	Blanc des Rosis	Vignis di Dolegna
Faralta	Conte di Cuccanea	Vinnaie
Franconia or Blaufränkisch	Engelwhite	Vino della Pace
L'Altromerlot	Gris	Vinograd Breg
Le Marne	Le Roverelle	Vintage Tunina
Montsclapade	Masarotte	Vitovska
Pignolo	Molamatta	
Plazate	Nuvizial	**Others**
Rivarossa	Picol	
Ronco dei Roseti	Ronc di Juri	Apicio, *W-Sw*
Ronco del Gnemiz	Ronco Blanchis	Moscato Rosa, *P-Sw*
Ronco della Torre	Ronco delle Acacie	Spumante Brut, *W/P-Dr-Sp*
Rosso de La Tour	Ronco delle Magnolie	
Rosso della Centa	Ronco di Corte	

Regional capital: Trento

Provinces: Bolzano (Bozen), Trento.

Trentino-Alto Adige ranks 11th among the regions in size (13,620 square kilometers) and 16th in population (880,000).

Vineyards cover 13,500 hectares (17th) of which registered DOC plots total 11,100 hectares (10th).

Annual wine production of 1,200,000 hectoliters (13th) includes 61% or 730,000 hectoliters DOC (4th), of which about 70% is red.

*I*taly's northern most region with alpine borders on Austria and Switzerland is split into two distinct provinces. Trentino, around the city of Trento to the south, is historically Italian in language and culture. Alto Adige, around the city of Bolzano or Bozen to the north, is better known as Südtirol to the prominent German-speaking population. The South Tyrol, historically part of Austria, is officially bilingual.

Walled in by the Rhaetian Alps and the Dolomites, only about 15 percent of Trentino-Alto Adige's land is cultivable and much that is produces fruit and wine grapes. The difficulty of training vines over wooden pergolas on hillside terraces compels growers to emphasize quality. More than 60% of production is DOC and some 35% of the wine is exported (both Italy's highest rates). Yet, though experts agree that the alpine climate favors grapes for perfumed white wines, the focus remains on reds, which account for more than two-thirds of the region's production.

The dominant variety is Schiava or Vernatsch, source of lightweight reds that flow north prodigiously to German-speaking countries. The most highly regarded of these is St. Magdalener or Santa Maddalena, grown on the picturesque slopes overlooking Bolzano. The best known is Caldaro or Kalterersee, produced from vines around the pretty lake of that name at the rate of more than 20 million liters a year, which puts it high among Italy's DOCs in volume. But the ranks of roseate ruby wines from Schiava extend through the South Tyrol along the Adige river into Trentino and the Veneto under the Val d'Adige appellation.

Other reds can show greater class. Alto Adige's native Lagrein and Trentino's Teroldego stand with northern Italy's most distinguished vines, making wines of singular personality. Marzemino makes a fresh, lively red for casual sipping. Considerable space is devoted to Cabernet and Merlot, which occasionally reach impressive heights both alone and in blends. The region also produces some of Italy's finest rosé, perhaps the most impressive being Lagrein Kretzer. The sweet Moscato Rosa with its gracefully

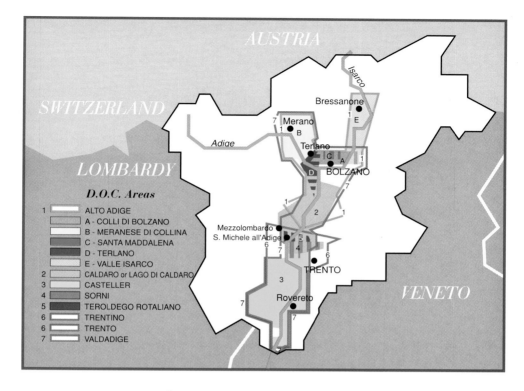

D.O.C. Areas

1	ALTO ADIGE
A	COLLI DI BOLZANO
B	MERANESE DI COLLINA
C	SANTA MADDALENA
D	TERLANO
E	VALLE ISARCO
2	CALDARO or LAGO DI CALDARO
3	CASTELLER
4	SORNI
5	TEROLDEGO ROTALIANO
6	TRENTINO
6	TRENTO
7	VALDADIGE

flowery aroma is a rare and prized dessert wine.

The growing demand for white wine has influenced growers to plant more of the international premium varieties. The heights are favorable for aromatic whites: Gewürztraminer, Sylvaner, Müller Thurgau and white Moscato. But the quality of Chardonnay, Pinot Bianco and Grigio, Sauvignon and Riesling Renano from certain cellars can also stand with Italy's finest. Trentino's native Nosiola makes fine dry white and is also the base of Vino Santo, a rich dessert wine from the Valle dei Laghi.

Production of the numerous varietal wines is centered in two large DOC zones: Trentino in the south and Alto Adige or Südtiroler in the north. Valdadige applies to red and white wines of popular commercial standards produced between Merano and Verona.

Several small DOC zones are noted for class. Valle d'Isarco and Terlano produce some exquisite whites in Alto Adige, and Santa Maddalena has a long-standing reputation for its refined light red. Teroldego, grown on the Rotaliano plain north of Trento, is an unusually attractive red when young, with capacity to age splendidly from good vintages.

Although the region's white wines are often considered light by international standards, some have an unexpected propensity to

age. Pinot Bianco, Gewürztraminer, Riesling and Müller Thurgau have been known to remain fresh and vital for a decade or two. But the emphasis is on popularly priced Pinot Grigio, Chardonnay and Pinot Bianco which can offer outstanding values.

Ultimately, producers in both provinces have been making whites of greater weight and complexity — in particular from Chardonnay, Sauvignon and the Pinots and also from Sylvaner, Riesling, Müller Thurgau and Gewürztraminer, whose name derives from the South Tyrolean village of Tramin. A few are also working with new techniques on red wines, notably in combinations of Cabernet and Merlot, but also with Pinot Nero and the underrated Lagrein. They are gradually enhancing the status of a region whose sterling record with DOC doesn't fully express its extraordinary quality potential.

Trentino, which boasts Italy's largest production of Chardonnay, is a leader with sparkling wines by the classical method, spumante that may qualify under the trademark of Trento Classico. Alto Adige has also stepped up sparkling wine production. Despite the traditional flow north, Trentino-Alto Adige's wines - whites especially - have been making steady progress in Italy and, just recently, on more distant markets, such as the United States and United Kingdom.

DOCs (8)*

Alto Adige or Südtiroler	24 types plus 5 subdenominations: Cabernet/Cabernet Franc/Cabernet Sauvignon *R-Dr*, Rs Ag-2; Cabernet Lagrein *R-Dr*, Rs Ag-2; Cabernet-Merlot *R-Dr*, Rs Ag-2; Chardonnay *W-Dr*; Lagrein Dunkel or Scuro *R-Dr*, Rs Ag-2; Lagrein Kretzer or Rosato *P-Dr*; Malvasia or Malvasier *R-Dr*; Merlot *R-Dr*, Rs Ag-2; Merlot Rosato or Kretzer *P-Dr*; Moscato Giallo or Goldenmuskateller *W-Sw*; Moscato Rosa or Rosenmuskateller *P-Sw*; Müller Thurgau or Riesling-Sylvaner *W-Dr*; Pinot Bianco or Weissburgunder *W-Dr*, also *Sp*; Pinot Grigio or Ruländer *W-Dr*, also *Sp*; Pinot Nero or Blauburgunder *R-Dr*, Rs Ag-2; Pinot Nero Rosato or Blauburgunder Kretzer *P-Dr*; Riesling Italico or Welschriesling *W-Dr*; Riesling Renano or Rheinriesling *W-Dr*; Sauvignon *W-Dr*; Schiava Grigia or Grauvernatsch *R-Dr*; Schiave or Vernatsch *R-Dr*; Spumante *W-P-Dr-Sp*; Sylvaner *W-Dr*; Traminer Aromatico or Gewürztraminer *W-Dr*; **Colli di Bolzano or Bozner Leiten** *R-Dr*; **Meranese di Collina or Meraner Hügel** *R-Dr*; **Santa Maddalena or St. Magdalener** *R-Dr*; **Terlano or Terlaner** (8 types: Chardonnay *W-Dr*; Müller Thurgau *W-Dr*; Pinot Bianco or Weissburgunder *W-Dr*; Riesling Italico or Welschriesling *W-Dr*; Riesling Renano or Rheinriesling *W-Dr*; Sauvignon *W-Dr*; Sylvaner *W-Dr*; Terlano or Terlaner *W-Dr*, all also *Sp*); **Valle Isarco or Eisacktaler** (7 types: Kerner *W-Dr*; Klausner Leitacher *R-Dr*; Müller Thurgau *W-Dr*; Pinot Grigio or Ruländer *W-Dr*; Sylvaner *W-Dr*; Traminer Aromatico or Gewürztraminer *W-Dr*; Veltliner *W-Dr*.)
Caldaro or Lago di Caldaro or Kalterersee	*R-Dr*
Casteller	*R-Dr*, also *Sw*
Sorni	*R-W-Dr*
Teroldego Rotaliano	*R-Dr*, Rs Ag-2, also *P-Dr*

Trentino	20 types: Bianco *W-Dr*; Cabernet *R-Dr*, Rs Ag-2; Cabernet Franc *R-Dr*, Rs Ag-2; Cabernet Sauvignon *R-Dr*, Rs Ag-2; Chardonnay *W-Dr*, also *Sp*; Lagrein *R-P-Dr*, Rs (R) Ag-2; Marzemino *R-Dr*, Rs Ag-2; Merlot *R-Dr*, Rs Ag-2; Moscato Giallo *W-Sw*, also *Ft*; Moscato Rosa *P-Sw*, also *Ft*; Müller Thurgau *W-Dr*; Nosiola *W-Dr*; Pinot Bianco *W-Dr*, also *Sp*; Pinot Grigio *W-Dr*, also *Sp*; Pinot Nero *R-Dr*, Rs Ag-2, also *W-P-Dr-Sp*; Riesling Italico *W-Dr*; Riesling Renano *W-Dr*; Rosso *R-Dr*; Traminer Aromatico *W-Dr*; Vino Santo *W-Sw*, also Liquoroso *W-Sw-Ft*, Ag-3
Trento	*W-P-Dr-Sp*, Rs (W) Ag-3
Valdadige or Etschtaler	7 types: Bianco *W-Dr*, also *Sw*; Chardonnay *W-Dr*; Pinot Bianco *W-Dr*; Pinot Grigio *W-Dr*, also *Sw*; Rosato *P-Dr*, also *Sw*; Rosso *R-Dr*, also *Sw*; Schiava *R-Dr*

* Note: names and labels in Alto Adige or Südtiroler may be in Italian or German

OTHER WINES OF NOTE

Red-Dry	Rebo	Palai
Castel Schwanburg	Rosso di Pila	Stravino di Stravino
Conte Federico	San Leonardo	Vigna Piccola
Cornelius	Tebro	Villa Margon
Foianeghe Rosso	**White-Dry**	**Others**
Fratagranda		
Granato	Castel San Michele Bianco	Essenzia, *W-Sw/Dr*
Grener	De Vite	Kerner, *P-Dr*
Linticlarus	Fayé	Pregiato, *P-Sw*
Mori Vecio	Feldmarschall	Trento Classico, *W-Dr-Sp*
Navesel	Foianeghe Bianco	Vin dei Molini, *P-Dr*
Norico	Luna dei Feldi	
Pragiara	Müller Thurgau di Faedo	

"The main thing to remember about Italian cuisine," a Florentine maestro begins his cooking classes for foreigners, "is that it doesn't exist. First, because the term cuisine is French, but more important because in my country, thank heaven, we have no uniform way of cooking".

He might have added that "Northern Italian cuisine" was invented abroad, apparently to indicate restaurants that do not serve *pizza napoletana* or spaghetti with meatballs smothered in tomato sauce. To suggest anything more than distant links between the regional dishes of northern Italy — the braised meats and creamy risottos of Piedmont, the fish and herb-inspired touches of Liguria, the pasta and pork delicacies of Emilia or schnitzel and dumpling fare of the South Tyrol, for instance — is little short of heresy. The same could be said of the southern regions where, however, the flavors of the Mediterranean remain generally more intact than elsewhere.

On analysis, *la cucina Italiana* is a miscellany of regional, provincial, local and family dishes that vary from season to season and cook to cook. It is a deliciously random fund of little treasures, of recipes rarely written down but passed intuitively from one generation to another, modified according to the produce available and enhanced by knowing hands.

What sets the cooking of Italy apart from that of any other country is the variety of ingredients and spontaneity of the preparation. In places you can find the Mediterranean diet at its purest in extra virgin olive oil with pasta or bread, fresh herbs, vegetables and fruit, fish and cheese, and wine from the nearest hillside. But you can also find some of the richest fare of Europe with sauces based on butter and cream, meat patés, beef, pork, poultry and game, lush pastries and sweets, and wine lists that carry grand old vintages from different regions. It depends on the time and place, of course, but wherever you dine in Italy expect to be surprised.

Still, there is no denying that some Italian cooks have attempted to standardize the fare. You can find *spaghetti alla carbonara* on menus in Milan and *costoletta alla milanese* in Rome, *peperonata* in Verona and *polenta* in Palermo. All healthy citizens eat pasta in some form regularly and nearly every village north and south has a pizzeria. But the variations from place to place are infinite, and as any gastronome worth his *Parmigiano* will insist, you have to travel to the place of origin to taste the foods and wines of Italy together at their authentic best.

Cognoscenti will tell you that the ultimate in *fonduta con tartufi* is prepared around Alba in Piedmont and served with a local Dolcetto. The best *pasta con le sarde* is made around Messina and matched with a white from Etna. For *zampone con lenticchie* it's Modena and a dry Lambrusco di Sorbara; *risi e bisi,* it's Venice with a Tocai from Lison or Friuli's hills; *trenette col pesto,* it's Genoa and the little known white Lumassina; *ossobuco con risotto alla milanese,* it's Milan and Barbera from Oltrepò Pavese; *tagliatelle con ragù,* it's Bologna and a youthful Sangiovese di Romagna; *bistecca alla fiorentina and fagioli,* it's Florence and robust Chianti Classico. And, of course, for *pizza napoletana,* it's Naples with a fresh, young white or rosé from Vesuvius or Ischia.

A typical Italian meal may range through three to five dishes, sometimes more. But let's consider the prime courses of *antipasti* (appetizers), *primi* (pastas, risottos or soups), *secondi* (main courses, usually meat, poultry or fish) and *formaggi* (cheeses) with some further suggestions for vegetables, fruit and dessert. Here are some matches of foods and wines that complement each other. Still, despite what you might have heard about obligatory matches of local dishes with local vintages, the food of Italy is usually admirably adaptable and so, naturally enough, are the wines. So experiments with other combinations are encouraged.

ANTIPASTI	*WINES*
Asparagi al burro e parmigiano (asparagus with butter and Parmesan)	Müller Thurgau or Sylvaner Alto Adige
Bruschetta (grilled bread with garlic and olive oil)	Vernaccia di San Gimignano
Crostini di fegato (chicken liver paté on crisp bread)	Chianti Colli Fiorentini
Fiori di zucchini fritti (fried zucchini flowers)	Orvieto Classico
Frutti di mare (poached or raw seafood salad)	Verdicchio dei Castelli di Jesi
Gamberi or scampi bolliti (poached giant shrimp or prawns)	Soave Classico
Mozzarella in carrozza (breaded and fried Mozzarella-anchovy sandwich)	Greco di Tufo
Ostriche (raw oysters)	Gavi

Peperonata (stewed peppers)	Regaleali Rosato
Pizzette (pizza slices with herbs or cheeses)	Castel del Monte Rosato
Prosciutto con melone or fichi (prosciutto with cantaloupe or figs)	Bianco di Scandiano (dry)

PRIMI	*WINES*
Bucatini all'amatriciana (thick spaghetti pipes with bacon, pepper)	Montepulciano d'Abruzzo Cerasuolo
Cannelloni al forno (pasta rolls with meat sauce and bechamel)	Rosso Piceno Superiore
Crespelle con ricotta e spinaci (crêpes with ricotta - spinach filling)	Chardonnay Alto Adige or Trentino
Fettuccine al burro (egg noodles with butter, cream, Parmesan)	Frascati Superiore
Gnocchi di patate con ragù (potato dumplings with meat sauce)	Franciacorta Bianco
Minestrone (thick vegetable soup)	Vermentino Riviera Ligure di Ponente
Orecchiette con cime di rapa (ear-shaped pasta with turnip greens, garlic, peppers)	Locorotondo
Pasta e fagioli (pasta with beans)	Merlot Isonzo or Grave del Friuli
Ravioli (envelopes with a meat or spinach filling)	Grignolino d'Asti
Ribollita (thick vegetable and bread soup or stew)	Chianti Colli Senesi
Risotto alla parmigiana (cooked with broth and Parmesan)	Bianco di Custoza
Spaghetti alla carbonara (with salt pork, eggs and cheese)	Marino Superiore

Spaghetti con le vongole (with tiny clams)	Corvo Bianco
Tortellini in brodo (small pasta rings in chicken broth	Albana di Romagna (dry)
Zuppa di pesce (fish soup)	Rosé di Bolgheri

SECONDI	**WINES**
Abbachio or agnello alla romana (lamb with rosemary, garlic, anchovies)	Pinot Nero Alto Adige or Colli Orientali del Friuli
Brasato al Barolo (beef braised in Barolo)	Barolo
Branzino al forno (baked sea bass)	Tocai Friulano Collio
Carpaccio (paper-thin slices of veal, mushrooms, Parmesan)	Riviera del Garda Bresciano Rosso
Costoletta alla milanese (breaded veal cutlet)	Barbera d'Asti
Fegato alla Veneziana (calf's liver sautéed with onions)	Cabernet di Pramaggiore or Piave
Fritto misto di pesce (fried shrimp, squid and other fresh fish)	Bianco d'Alcamo
Melanzane alla parmigiana (stewed eggplant with Mozzarella, Parmesan)	Rosato di Salento
Pollo alla diavola (charcoal grilled chicken)	Valpolicella Classico Superiore
Saltimbocca alla romana (veal fillet sautéed with prosciutto and sage)	Rosso Conero
Scampi alla griglia (grilled sea prawns)	Sauvignon Colli Orientali del Friuli
Stracotto alla fiorentina (Florentine beef stew)	Chianti Classico or Vino Nobile di Montepulciano
Trota al burro (trout roasted in butter)	Lugana
Vitello tonnato (cold veal slices with tuna sauce)	Spumante brut metodo classico

FORMAGGI / WINES

Opinions vary on which wine to serve with which cheese, and since Italy has more than 400 types of cheeses this is only a general guideline.

Mild soft cheeses, such as Bel Paese, Caprino, Fior di Latte, Mozzarella or Ricotta	Light to medium-bodied whites, such as Orvieto, Frascati, Soave, Lugana, Albana di Romagna, Corvo Bianco, Pinot Grigio, Sauvignon, Riesling
Lightly ripened or seasoned cheeses, such as Fontina, Groviera, fresh Caciotta or Pecorino, Toma or Tuma, Taleggio, Robiola or young Provolone	Rosés or light reds, such as Caldaro, Bardolino, Riviera del Garda Chiaretto, Castel del Monte Rosato, Dolcetto d'Alba, Grignolino, Merlot, young Chianti
Ripe or aged cheese, such as Parmigiano-Reggiano, Grana Padano, Pecorino Toscano or Umbro, Asiago, sweet Gorgonzola, Castelmagno or Caciocavallo	Robust reds, such as Barbaresco, Barolo, Barbera d'Asti Superiore, Brunello di Montalcino, Torgiano Rosso Riserva,Taurasi, Aglianico del Vulture,Valtellina Superiore or Cabernet
Sharp, peppered or very ripe cheeses, such as Provolone Piccante, Pecorino Romano or Sardo, Bitto or sharp Gorgonzola.	Choices may vary from dry but rich reds such as Amarone, Sfursat, Sagrantino di Montefalco or Primitivo di Manduria to dry fortified wines such as Marsala Vergine or Vernaccia di Oristano to sweet wines such as Recioto di Soave, Vin Santo, Aleatico or Malvasia.

VERDURA

The wine to serve with most vegetable dishes depends on whether they are a main course or a side dish, in which case the fish, meat or poultry would determine the choice. Most vegetable dishes alone call for a wine on the light side—a white, rosé or easy red. Some, like asparagus and spinach, are hard to match and others, like artichokes or salad with vinegar, are pratically impossible—better without wine.

FRUTTA

Italians usually eat fruit fresh and without a specific wine to accompany, though lightly sweet and bubbly Moscato or Malvasia go nicely with many things.

DOLCI

Desserts can create problems, since Italy has both an astonishing variety of sweets and nearly as many sweet wines, many of them scarcely known abroad. There are some traditional matches: Tuscan almond biscuits with Tuscan Vin Santo, zabaglione and Marsala, and Milan's Christmas cake panettone with Asti Spumante. As a rule, lightly sweet desserts go best with lightly sweet wines, so fruit tarts, pound cakes, fruit sorbets and pastries might be matched with Moscato d'Asti or Verduzzo Friulano or a Malvasia from Colli Piacentini or Sardinia. Richer sweets take sweeter or stronger wines, such as Marsala Superiore Garibaldi Dolce or Malvasia delle Lipari or Moscato Passito di Pantelleria. Sweets laced with chocolate, rum, candied fruit or spices such as ginger or cinnamon are usually too much for wine.

D

E

P

R